This "thing" of running a vehicle off the road for "grins, " just to get away from it all, or to compete in the steadily increasing number of off-road racing events has to be one of the most exhilarating experiences in the motor vehicle's relatively short history.

For those of you who are not a part of the Southern California "scene, " perhaps a bit of history would serve well before you begin digging into the following pages. Shortly before World War II, a handful of motorcyclists began spending their weekends zipping around in the desert area near Los Angeles. From this evolved the American version of Enduros and Cross Country or Hare and Hound racing. Before the gang hung up their helmets to become better acquainted with Uncle Sam, several of each type of event had been held in the Southern California desert.

Concurrent with this was the development of dune buggies, which in the beginning were just that. Cutdown versions of older-model American cars chugged around the sand dunes at Pismo Beach, California, and Yuma, Arizona. Save for an occasional "grudge race" up the side of a dune, there were no competitive events.

During that war, two things of significance to this type of activity occurred. Those inclined toward the two wheelers became better acquainted with the lighter, faster and easy-to-handle European motorcycles. GIs also came to know a ubiquitous, slab-sided, underpowered military vehicle called the Jeep.

At the end of that war, motorcyclists went back out to their fun and games in the deserts; lighter and faster bikes were first imported and then built in this country, and the sport of riding a motorcycle off the road in competition or just for weekend pleasure mushroomed out of sight. At

Volkswagenwerke wouldn't believe what's happened to this sedan. Clever work and careful planning with shears and cutting torch has transformed this bug into an all-out road racer. The money saved by not buying a glass body has been reinvested into good things like the roll cage. Lights and air cleaner will be wiped out, however, should this machine "get on its head."

the same time, more and more Jeeps began showing up in the boonies. More often than not, the flathead four-cylinder engine had been replaced with a healthier engine. The practice of cutting down old cars for running on the sand dunes, and later the desert, increased because everyone and his brother had some kind of old car they had kept alive during that war. At trade-in time the cars were worth little, so why not cut off the body, move the engine back and have a no-cost weekend toy? Scores of automotive enthusiasts did just that and the "science" of running off the road began to catch on.

Then one day, some unknown soul drove a VW sedan onto the sand and the automotive world has never been quite the same. That is what this book is about. The discovery that a VW outfitted with large tires for flotation could negotiate all but the steepest dunes led to a number of steps in rapid order. The sedan body was removed and this lightweight number began giving the boys a ride as nothing else ever had. In 1963, an energetic and sharp-minded "beach bum, " Bruce Meyers, designed a fiberglass body/chassis which used VW suspension, steering and engine/transaxle components. Subsequently, Meyers found that construction costs of his fiberglass body/chassis were too great for mass sales acceptance. So, he redesigned his "thing" into a fiberglass body which would fit directly onto a shortened VW floor pan. The dune buggy, as it is thought of today, was thus born.

Cruisin' with Corvair power, straight pipes and marshmallows for tires. The Corvair has enough low-end torque to spin those big tires over the top of a dune, making this a mean combination for the sand.

This Variant wagon never gets a rest. Big tires are bolted on for a weekend of fun at the beach. Stock tires go back on Sunday night and stay in place for grocery shopping, kid hauling and errand running. Rear engine mount hanging from bumper mounts is important to keep all of the engine's torque directed to the wheels.

Bottom: Functional fun for the dunes. Despite appearance, the straight-cut rear tires offer traction as well as flotation in the soft stuff. Flagged antenna is a must for warning others exactly where you are to avoid collisions when topping dunes.

Scores of imitators and thousands of customers have seen to it that a dune buggy has been just about everywhere at one time or another.

There are shortcomings to this type of car of course, but this can be expected from equipment which is so specialized in function.

Far more important than the minor shortcomings are the recreational advantages of owning and using a VW-based off-road vehicle. The list is a long one: low cost, availability of parts (stock and custom), ease of maintenance, and "go-anywhere ability" to provide countless hours of fun for an individual or family.

This book tells you how to go about preparing a VW-based vehicle for safe and dependable off-road use. Throughout the volume, constant reference is made to modifications relative to vehicles prepared for competition. Although you may never plan to race, keep in mind that it is the performance-minded enthusiasts who have very quickly discovered how to correct the weak points of a vehicle being taken off the road. In other words, the modifications and suggestions relative to race vehicles are also applicable to the "fun car" which you are preparing for weekend outings with the family.

Dig in--and have fun!

Undiluted, first-class fun. As soon as you get back home from any beach running, flush the underside with plenty of fresh water because salt water can eat through a floor pan before you've finished trying to wear the car out. This also wrecks the starter and any slip connections in the electrical system.

The purpose behind building up a VW-based vehicle to take off the road is just that: to take off the road for exploring, camping and just generally for "grins." As every camper, Jeeper or woodsman will tell you, there's plenty out there for us all to enjoy, but first we must do a number of things correctly before the enjoyment comes. The inexperienced can get into a lot of trouble, with or without a vehicle, out away from civilization. If you are in the category of the inexperienced, admit it, start learning and begin having fun.

Thought-out, deliberate action coupled with common sense is a very hard combination to beat. Start working on it. For instance, you should know that the vehicle is in excellent mechanical condition before ever turning off the pavement. You should have checked all tires for cuts, gouges or sticks imbedded in the rubber. The battery should be fully charged. A small, home-type battery charger is a wise investment and can save a lot of grief. Do you have enough gasoline to go where you want to go and get back? You'd be surprised how many people run out of gasoline out in the middle of nowhere. On a vehicle with no gas gauge, make a graduated measuring stick and check the level often. On the first several outings, whether short or long, keep careful tabs on distance traveled and gas consumed. We've seen several graduated gas measuring sticks marked off in gallons and miles that could be traveled on remaining fuel. Not dead accurate perhaps, but of more help than a blank look on your face.

At least one quart of extra oil should be kept in the vehicle at all times. For a vehicle going very far, three quarts is a minimum. Always be prepared for the unexpected. What happens if you roll the sedan over while moving down into a dry wash? You were practically stopped when the vehicle tipped over. No one is hurt. You and a friend were strapped tightly to the seats, laughing and scrambling over each other trying to get out. Save for some scratches and some shoved-in fenders, the car is not hurt. But, the oil has drained out. This is no problem if you have the extra oil.

Obviously you cannot carry a spare of every part which might break on an off-road vehicle, but you can take steps to ensure that you'll ride back and not walk. What happens if the throttle linkage is broken off by a cactus or rock when you roll over or have some other mishap? With some imagination, air-conditioning duct tape, mechanic's wire and a pair of pliers, the linkage is repaired.

As you drive, try to file small bits of information away that might be needed later. Did you just pass an old campsite? An excellent place to

FUN — in Safety

This lightweight sand runner is down to the bare essentials but still carries a good collection of tools lashed down with tape and elastic tie down cord.

Apparently, this car sees limited time off the road. Stock air cleaner, street recapped tires, and a skid plate which fails to protect valve covers are indications that the driver has not planned to go off-road seriously. Skid plate should not be mounted to back of engine.

As you mount gas tanks, route fuel lines, and justify leaving out the fire extinguisher, refer back to these sobering scenes. This sleek fiberglass-bodied buggy had a proud, but extinguisher-less owner. Keep an extinguisher in your sedan or buggy!

look for a coat hanger or other wire to be used in making repairs. Need a tin can or block of wood? How far back? Again, this can save time and a lot of thrashing around. An extra set of points, a distributor cap, and a fuel pump are small but worthwhile items to be packed into the vehicle for longer runs, together with an extra set of plugs and a couple of plug wires and connectors. The duct tape, wire and a few hand tools are bare essentials. Remember that if a fuel pump quits, it does no good to have a spare without tools to install it. With tools and spares laid out on the garage floor behind the engine, make a dry run to see if you are prepared in case this, that or the other had to be done. A good adjustable wrench may save taking several wrenches, but it is worthless if it cannot be maneuvered into place on a nut or bolt. Spare parts and smaller tools can be wrapped with several mechanic's shop rags and tied into a bundle with some wire or several feet of 1/4-inch ID Neoprene or rubber fuel line which can be used as a siphon. Take a medium-size ball-peen hammer. Tape it to the lower roll bar support or saw the handle short and shove it in the glove compartment, or give it to the co-driver to play with--but take a hammer. We've heard it said that anything can be fixed with Vise-Grips, duct tape and a hammer. This might be stretching the facts a little, but we've seen some shaky and crude repairs that kept someone from walking home.

Ted Trevor, who is quick to point out that "Somewhere there's a rock with your name on it," suggests that you include bailing wire in your repair kit, "because it has more tensile strength than duct tape."

How about this one? A fist-sized hole was ripped into the bottom of the transaxle by a rock (no skid plate). The vehicle was far enough down the Baja peninsula that a couple of days could easily slip by without seeing another human. What to do? The repair was made with shop rags wrapped about a small rock shoved against the hole and held in place with a split tin can covered by duct tape and then wrapped with wire.

Perhaps not needed was the adobe (mud and straw) patch that was then placed over all this to minimize the amount of lube that might seep out through the rags. Of course, when the hole was torn, all the oil drained out so engine oil was used along with a small can of gooey additive. The oil can was too large to fit over the filler hole in the transaxle case so this had to be siphoned in. The "goo" was dribbled along a stick and routed into the filler hole. More lube was added when a small village was reached. The adobe patch began falling apart but the vehicle was driven slowly more than 300 miles without further repairs.

Despite what you may have done to the front spindles to strengthen them, one may break. If this happens, pinch the brake line or hammer it closed ahead of the flex line. Unscrew or cut the flex brake line and remove the backing plate assembly because it only adds weight where it is not needed. Also, it will hang down and drag. Remove one of the large tires from the rear and place it on the remaining front spindle or put a large spare on the remaining spindle. We're after flotation here. Shift all weight possible away from the broken front end. This may mean that the passengers get to ride in the back seat or maybe perch on a rear fender or nerf bar and hang on to whatever happens to be handy in an effort to keep the broken spindle off the ground. Drive slowly. This procedure is not uncommon and many a mile has been negotiated in just this manner by three-wheel sedans and buggies.

Spend time thinking about creature comforts inside your off-road car. Would a grab bar across the dash be helpful to a passenger? Should the lower edge of the dash be padded? Should the seats be shoved further to the rear? Would a seat offering more side support be of aid on long trips? All this may seem trivial, but if you start banging a knee into a gutted steel door for four hundred miles, you'll not think it trivial. Seat belts are a must, and not just for safety's sake. That's reason enough, but they keep you in the seat instead of bouncing and banging around constantly. Buckle 'em up and leave 'em tight.

If children are to be riding off the road with you, give some special thought to their needs. If they are unhappy with the situation, you can bet that you'll be doubly unhappy. Naturally, they like to see what's going on, so make sure they can see where you're taking them. This is easy in an open buggy, but in a sedan a booster seat might have to be added. Children should be strapped into place. Figure out where they would go or what will happen if you suddenly slam on the brakes or have to whip sharply to either side. Foam rubber padding in the area of the rear side windows might be indicated here.

The prudent move, whether you are experienced or inexperienced, is to go off the road with another vehicle. This just makes good sense. Four men can move a car when two men can't budge it. Parts can be borrowed from one vehicle to help another along. The combinations are endless. By sticking with another vehicle off the road the prospects of having serious trouble are practically nil.

There is one danger, or potential danger, in going off the road with another vehicle. If the driver of the other vehicle is experienced and you are not, you can get into trouble by attempting to keep up. Cool it. When you overextend yourself, the possibility of a wreck or component breakage when running off the road reaches a certainty very quickly. Never drive further than you can see. Those who "cheat" and violate this little rule have to pay for it sooner or later. If you once drive further than you can see ("over your head," as the saying goes), it only encourages you to do more and more of it. Sooner or later there will be a rock, tree, gully or whatever right where it should not be.

Never be ashamed to stop the car, get out and walk over a particularly tricky area. You can "feel" the terrain out. Perhaps you can move a rock here or there or check to see if there is a huge hole or rock on the far side of the bush that you had planned to just skirt. While out of the car, walk around it. Is a tire low? Have you bent a rim? Is a fender torn and will it cut a tire? A small problem now can be a very big problem a little later on.

Perhaps we've been a little bit heavy on this talk about common sense. But the Volkswagen is a product of the common-sense approach and it just seems that a great amount of pleasure could be derived from the vehicle in its various forms by anyone who shared in that type of thinking.

"Bandido" by FUNCO is a typical off-road vehicle which can be purchased in any stage from bare kit through Baja-ready form.

Front Suspension

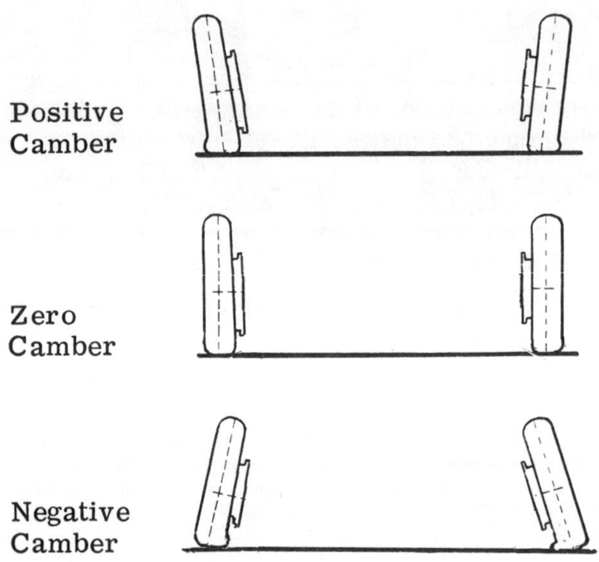

Crown Manufacturing in Newport Beach, California invented quick-steering arm extensions for the VW. These bolt-on spacers change the stock steering ratio to 1⅞ turns lock-to-lock. Turning radius of the vehicle is not altered, only the number of turns lock-to-lock on the steering wheel.

Suspension components take a beating off the road as they do in no other type of motoring. The modifying, replacement and treatment of VW components is the basis of hundreds of "bench-racing sessions" whenever enthusiasts meet. The problems in the discussion arise when one or more, and sometimes all, of the conversationalists don't understand what they are hearing, or in many cases don't know what they are talking about. Because suspension components on domestic and foreign cars give long and trouble-free service when driven normally on the street, all too few automotive enthusiasts are familiar with suspension nomenclature.

Don't feel like the Lone Ranger if you admit to a bit of confusion in the area of suspension dynamics, because many automotive engineers get lost when the angles and oscillations start changing. But we needn't go that deep into the subject to prepare a VW-based car for off the road. A basic understanding of certain terms is necessary to present a meaningful discussion of what to expect off the road.

Camber is one of three measurements and descriptions of wheel orientation. Simply, camber tells us whether the wheel leans toward or away from the center of the car. As shown in the drawing, camber is generally described as zero, positive, or negative. In operation, camber may change between the three attitudes mentioned above due to uneven terrain or the vehicle leaning to one side during cornering.

Caster is an angle from vertical (front to rear) of a line drawn through the kingpin, or in the case of a ball-joint suspension — through the ball joints. This angle is used to provide self-centering of the wheels, or steering stability. The kingpin (or ball joint) inclination is usually approximately three to five degrees. The top of the kingpin or top ball joint is towards the rear of the car.

Toe refers to the direction the wheel is headed with respect to the centerline of the vehicle. If the wheel is headed exactly parallel to the longitudinal axis of the car, then the attitude is referred to as zero toe. If the wheel is headed toward the center line extended from the front of the vehicle, then the attitude is toe-in. It follows that toe-out refers to a wheel pointed away from the center line. Changes in toe setting can be effected by turning the steering wheel or from deflections in the suspension or steering linkage (as in hitting a rock).

If tie rods are not correctly aligned with respect to the pitman and steering arms, "toe steer" and track changes due to large amounts of wheel travel in bump and rebound over rough terrain can create all kinds of mean handling problems.

"

Neutral-steer refers to the steering trait or characteristic of a vehicle which, when operating on a fixed radius, requires no change in the steering wheel angle to maintain the fixed radius regardless of speed changes. Neutral-steer and its kissin' cousins, over-steer and under-steer, are often misunderstood.

A vehicle is driven on a fixed radius on a flat surface at a carefully controlled speed. The speed is then increased--if the vehicle continues to circumscribe the same circle it did at the lower speed, then it is known to have neutral-steer. If the vehicle describes a larger circle with the increase in speed, then it is under-steering. If the vehicle points the nose into the circle with no change in the steering wheel, the vehicle is over-steering. Simplified still further, you might keep in mind that if you leave the road in a turn and the front end goes into the brush first, the car probably has under-steer. If the rear end goes into the tulies first, the car is probably an over-steering vehicle.

Although this fact may come as a surprise to many readers, most off-road vehicles exhibit both understeer AND oversteer, depending on lots of other variables, such as what the car is doing at that particular moment.

Basically, a nose-heavy, front-engine domestic sedan is set up to under-steer and the mid-engine race cars are set up for close to neutral-steer. This gets complicated in a hurry and we won't pursue the subject here, but the slip angle of the tires and a number of other factors determine steering characteristics, not merely front/rear weight distribution. What happens when the car is being driven, that is, kinetic or force distribution--is far more important than the at-rest weight distribution.

Hitting a large bump with the front of a car causes the front of the car to pitch upward, then as the rear wheels pass over the same obstruction, the rear end pitches upward and the front end is forced down. This up-and-down motion of a vehicle is generally referred to as pitch. Roll is the side-to-side, or leaning attitude, as in cornering, when the outside of the vehicle rolls down and the inside rolls up. Yaw refers to the turning of the vehicle in alternate directions about its vertical axis. A vehicle will yaw if driven perpendicular to a heavy wind, because aerodynamic lift on the body is greatly increased.

The preceding discussion of terms may help you to hold your own in the next bench-racing session.

Now, let's look at the Volkswagen's front suspension. It consists of two large steel tubes running across the chassis and enclosing torsion bars (springs). A trailing link is attached to each end of each torsion bar and these links in

Tube-chassis off-road car shows good placement of flexible brake line. It's up out of the way of brush. Tie rods have been beefed up with pipe. Hydraulic steering damper aids stability — is stock on later VWs. Steering box has been centered on torsion tube of this single-seater. Torsion-bar tube is braced to frame structure.

turn are attached to a king-pin link (on pre-66 cars). After '66 the torsion bar links end in ball joints attached directly to the spindle. A single hydraulic shock absorber is used for each wheel to the lower trailing arm at one end and to a "shock arm" which also holds the torsion tubes in correct alignment.

This entire unit of tubes, bars, shocks, spindles, steering box, tie rods, and (on the later models) hydraulic damper, may be unbolted from the VW chassis with either four or six bolts. The early, kingpin suspension models will have four bolts attaching the unit to the chassis and six bolts if the body is still installed. The other two bolts are body mounts which are located just in front of the gas tank. The clip on the steering shaft and the two flexible brake lines must also be disconnected. The unit is relatively low in cost, is rugged and versatile enough to be used for street and competition hot rods, in a formula (Formula V) of road-racing cars, and now, off the road. In short, the Volkswagen front-suspension unit is almost impossible to beat and requires only a minimum of modification in order to do battle off-road.

A trailing-arm suspension is particularly suited to rough roads because the arms move up and back (or away) from bumps as opposed to a solid-axle or A-arm suspension which transmits all energy more or less vertically. Despite full vertical wheel movement, there is no track change with the VW front end. All of this adds up to a rather comfortable ride and uncanny control at speed in the rough.

Before continuing, let us point out that the front ends can be interchanged if you weld on the

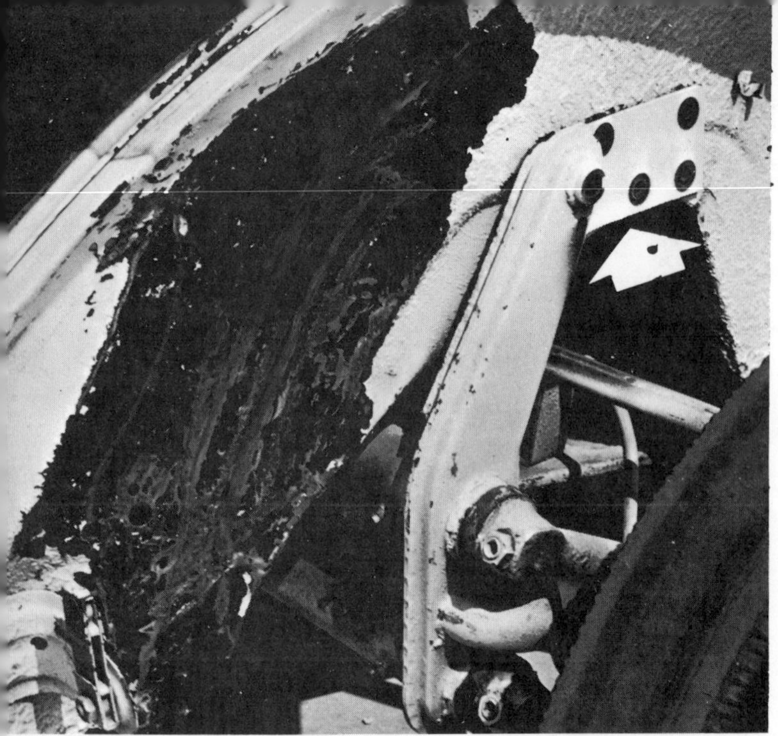

Described in the text, this method provides additional bracing for the front suspension unit to the sedan body. Tab is welded to the shock mount and bolted to inner panel. Shock mounting remains stock.

The steering-arm portion of the spindle can be beefed by welding in a section of plate. This should also be done on Porsche units used in place of the VW spindle.

appropriate frame head, which is available as a VW part. That is, a ball-joint front end can be bolted to a Volkswagen floor pan that left the factory with the king-pin-type front end. The reverse is also true.

KING PIN FRONT SUSPENSION - Trouble can be expected to show up in one of several areas when taking a VW suspension off the road. When nosing into a rock, tree or ditch, the two torsion tubes will sometimes move back. The bending point is at the inboard attachment points where the suspension unit bolts to the floor pan. The solution to the problem is just as obvious--constructing a brace outboard of the two stock mounting locations. On a sedan, the route most often taken is that of using the body structure for bracing. Weld a tab onto the inside rear of the shock mounting tower near the top. Shape the tab so it moves back to the wheel-well panel. Drill the tab so that it may be secured to the body panel with at least three 3/8-inch or 7/16-inch capscrews. Do this on both sides. Some enthusiasts prefer welding the tab to the inner fender panel. There is no advantage gained because a bolted tab is sufficiently strong if done correctly. A welded tab must be cut free of the torsion-tube assembly if the assembly is ever to be unbolted from the floor pan.

On a VW-based, fiberglass-bodied dune buggy, the problem of bending torsion tubes is no more severe than on a sedan, but the cure is somewhat more difficult. Square tubing may be welded to the inner top of each shock tower and then run back and down at 45 degrees to intersect with the outer edge of the floor pan. A tab is usually welded to the end of the tube and drilled for capscrew attachment to the floor-pan edge. Naturally, this is where the body is bolted onto the pan, so a hole has to be cut into the body to clear the brace. Most enthusiasts do not go to all this trouble--they either drive slower in the rough or suffer the consequences.

Before the torsion tubes bend, the long (left) tie rod, a steering arm or a spindle will usually

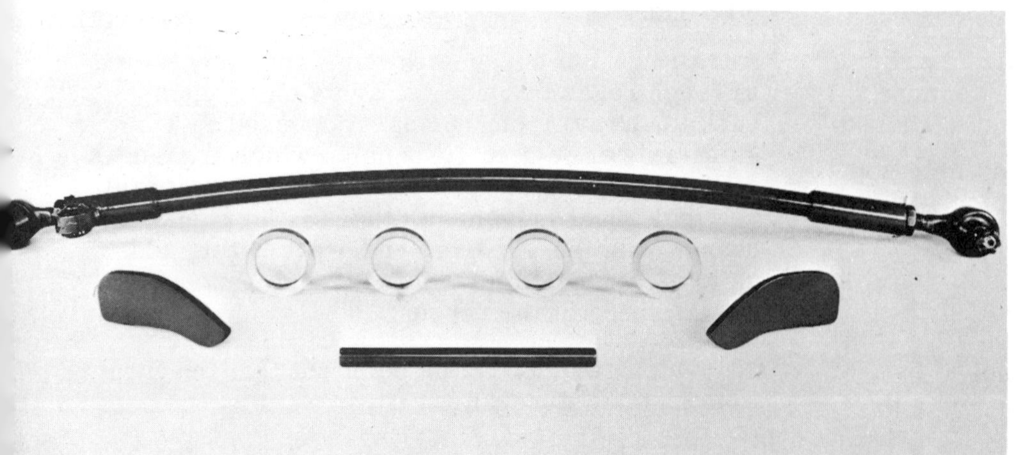

Crown Manufacturing's Beef-A-Steer kit has steel gussets for spindle-arm bracing, aluminum thrust washers to replace stock rubber seals between trailing arms and torsion tubes, and an internal stiffener for the short tie rod. Crown recommends using a short tie rod without the hole for the steering damper because this is also a weak point.

bend or break. In preparing a VW front suspension unit for off-road, the spindles should be replaced with new parts. Because you'll have to use a hydraulic press or large vise for this job, you might as well pick up a set of king pins and bushings at the parts counter--the cost is nominal and only a little more labor is involved. A stronger spindle which will interchange with the VW spindle is the Porsche of '61 to '63 vintage. This may be used if the Porsche bearing spacer is used along with the inner wheel bearing. There is a considerable difference in price between the VW and Porsche spindles, so you might be inclined to install new VW spindles and not go to the Porsche units until trouble developes. If you are not racing, chances are good that new VW units will suffice.

Porsche spindles bear P/N left 644 341 651 00, and right 644 341 652 00.

There are several ways of strengthening either the VW or Porsche spindle. Used together and executed correctly, the modifications produce a spindle which is many times more trouble free than a new stock VW spindle. In an effort to keep the spindle from bending, the spacer which absorbs thrust from the inner wheel bearing may be welded to the spindle flange. By welding this spacer (VW calls it a thrust washer) to the flange of the spindle at the section change, the load bearing area is effectively increased and the part can absorb increased loading with less change of failure. The weld must always be arced (heliarced if possible) with low-temperature stainless-steel rod. This welding may be done with the backing plate in place.

Spindle breakage is most common with the left spindle, probably because the left spindle is drilled for the speedometer cable. There is a method of curing this known as the Janowski Spindle Fix. It eliminates the speedometer and strengthens the spindle. Regardless of who (or what) Janowski is, the method of correction is sound and goes like this: hold the spindle in a lathe collett (1") and drill with 23/64" drill from the existing counterbore on the backside of the spindle to a depth within 3/4 inch of the outboard end. Ream the hole with a 0.374" reamer for the full depth which was drilled. Remove part from lathe and tap in a snug-fitting 3/8-inch dowel rod from the counterbored end so that you can hold the part in a 3-jaw chuck for tapping. This allows you to start the thread squarely by holding a 3/8-24 tap in the tailstock drill chuck. Finish tapping the hole and remove spindle from rod. This could be done with hand tools, but it's so simple to do it the right way that we'd have to recommend using the lathe. Clean and Loctite the threads, then screw in a socket-head capscrew which is 5-inches long under the head and which has had its head turned down to 0.480" to clear the counterbore. Torque to 160 foot pounds. Thank Janowski.

The steering-arm part of the spindle is easily braced by welding a small piece of 3/16-inch plate across the curved part of the steering arm. Do this to both right and left arms.

It should go without saying that if you plan to do anything with a vehicle based on the Volkswagen, you should have a VW technical manual close at hand. There are several on the market which

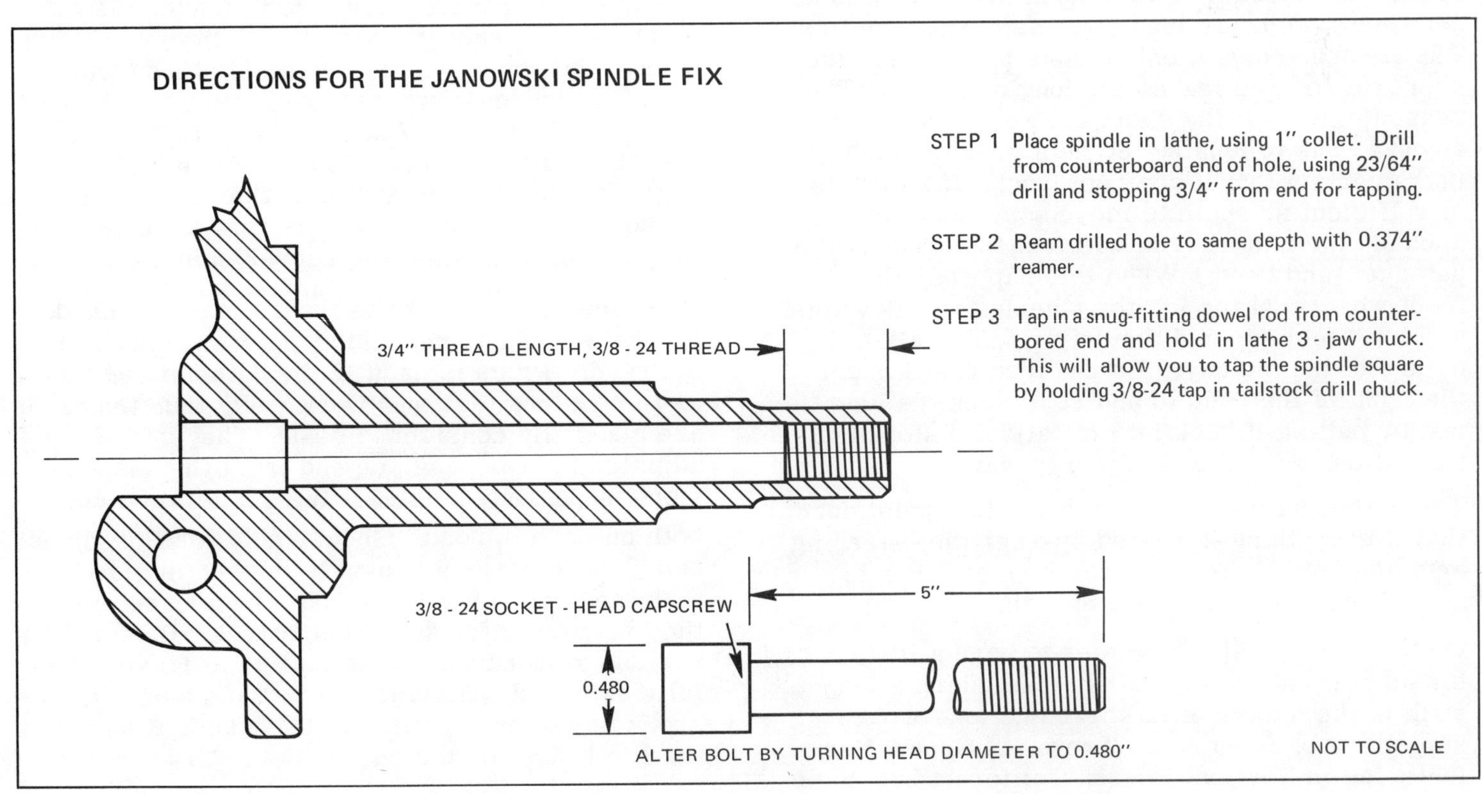

are quite good and can be used to guide even the novice through the routines of brake jobs, etc.

Which brings us to the point: do a brake job on the vehicle while the front end is all torn down for cleaning, inspection and bracing.

At this point a neat trick can be effected with very little effort. Unbolt the backing plate from the spindle. Holding the plate against the spindle in the stock location (with all brake apparatus removed), rotate the backing plate on the spindle 90 degrees to place the wheel cylinder (and thus brake line inlet) at the top. From the rear of the backing plate, mark where one and sometimes two holes must be drilled to rebolt the backing plate into this new position. Several more inches of protection from brush and rocks are thus given for the flexible brake line connecting the wheel cylinder with the steel line.

This seems to be a better idea, and just as effective as attaching clips and springs to the brake line and pulling it upward to achieve the same result. With either method of getting the line away from the ground, additional protection is easily gained by slipping a short length of 5/8-inch rubber hose over the line.

If properly lubricated, VW tie rod ends almost never bind up or break, but the tie rods themselves are not so reliable. There are two basic schools of thought on what to do to VW tie rods. One group advocates bracing both tie rods to the extent that they will not bend by welding on angle iron or covering them with a length of heavy-wall tubing. The other school of thought is somewhat more scientific, but due to the nature of the sport it is impossible to determine if the second solution is more or less successful than the first. The second group of enthusiasts braces only the short tie rod and leaves the long rod stock. Their reasoning is that the short rod resists bending anyway, due to length. So help it out more to make certain that it does not bend. If a blow is of sufficient strength to move some metal around, the long tie rod will feel the brunt of the damage--and bend. When this happens, the right front wheel will toe in, the steering will develop a "plow" feeling, and the driver will realize the nature of the malady. He can then crawl under the front of the vehicle and straighten the long tie rod by pulling it back into (relatively) stock configuration, and go on his merry way.

The enthusiasts advocating this action point out that if everything is beefed up--spindle, steering arm and both tie rods--something still has to give if the impact is great enough.

On the theory that it is better to have a little toe-in now and again, rather than taking a long walk in the middle of nowhere due to a broken something or other, Ted Trevor of Crown Manufacturing in Newport Beach, California has come up with an unusual kit. He calls it Beef-a-Steer. Basically, this consists of 3/4-inch spring steel torsion bar material which is tapped on both ends for the tie rods. Thus, when a heavy load is transferred to the rods via braced steering arms, these sections of the tie rod flex and then return or spring back into position. The kit also includes large aluminum collars which effectively increase the thrust surface of the trailing arms where they slip into the torsion tube needle bearings. These improve the front end action by taking out camber changes under severe side loadings.

Grease all fittings frequently. A machine being subjected to hard running off the road gets added loading and abrasive action from dirt and mud which leads to an early death for many components. Help out all you can with a heavy-duty grease. The same goes for repacking those wheel bearings which pick up sand and grit at alarming rates.

There are several other "tricks" to modifying VW front suspension units for off-road use. But they are of questionable virtue. The first such modification is to remove one or more leaves from the top torsion bar. This will in fact provide a somewhat softer ride but it will also allow the suspension to bottom--or reach the end of its travel--sooner. If the vehicle is to be used on fairly good secondary and paved roads, this might not be such a bad idea, especially on a glass-bodied car which is lighter than the steel-bodied sedan.

The rubber stop at each end of the torsion-tube assembly is often removed to allow slightly more vertical wheel travel. If there is fender clearance (certainly not enough on some buggies) and if you change the shock length, the steel stops can be cut off to increase wheel travel from 5-3/4 to almost 9-1/4 inches. Advantages include more travel, increased ground clearance and a steeper angle for the trailing arms. If the stop is left on, it should be heated and bent so that the upper arm is not resting against the rubber stop.

Most any of the shock absorbers manufactured for the VW front suspension work quite well off the road. Price is usually the determining factor as to how long they will work well, thus the Konis are generally considered best. They can also be adjusted by unbolting one end from the suspension--especially helpful if the car is to be run both on and off-road. Shocks sold for Porsches and Transporters are usually higher in price than the shocks for VW's, but check carefully, as they may not offer sufficient travel. Be sure that you use a shock which has sufficient travel when fully extended. If its travel is too short, the shock will soon destroy itself because it becomes the limit stop for the suspension. Crack!

On the early front ends--those with shocks having an eyelet at the upper end--a problem is
often encountered which brings tempers to a
boil in a hurry when attempting to install a new
set of shocks. The bolt, on which the upper end
of the shock mounts, is prone to rust and lock
up to the shock mounting bracket. Applying heat
is sometimes the only way that the bolt can be
loosened. Once having gone through the hassle
of getting the bolt out, many enthusiasts take a
half-inch drill motor in hand and ream out the
bolt hole in the upper shock mount. Then an
aircraft-quality bolt is used to bolt through the
mount instead of just into it. We recommend
making this "fix."

Large flat washer retainers should be used on
the outboard ends of rubber shock grommets,
thereby ensuring that the parts will not fall completely apart if the grommet fails.

The cross-over, anti-roll type, stabilizer bar
found on all the later VW's is usually removed
from the front suspension of buggies and sedans
that spend most of their lives off the road. The
stabilizer tends to make the vehicle plow and
somewhat sluggish at speed in loose terrain.
This stabilizer bar is simply clamped to both
lower torsion arms and may be easily removed,
easily reinstalled, too, if you discover that it is
desirable for your particular application.

The hydraulic steering damper found on the later
VWs, and also sold as an accessory for the
earlier models in auto-parts stores, cuts driver
fatigue and provides a sure, firm feel of the
road. It is especially helpful when traveling
rapidly in a rutted road or field which would
normally make the vehicle whip or veer from
side to side. For competition, some drivers
prefer to double up by including a hydraulic
damper on each tie rod. Vehicles subjected to off-
road beating can be made more responsive by replacing shocks and the steering damper. Koni has
a heavy-duty damper to fit all VW suspensions.
Some drivers don't like the dampers for the sand
because the damper causes loss of "feel." A rub-
ber-covered steering wheel also helps to cut
fatigue.

BALL-JOINT FRONT SUSPENSION - As stated
earlier, there is a myth in some circles that the
late, or ball-joint, front suspension units from a
VW just "won't cut it" off the road. The fact is
that there have been few that have seen service
off the road and fewer still that were maintained
by someone who had an appreciation and understanding of the unit.

All the modifications listed previously for the
king pin-type suspension apply, except that of

Left front VW spindle is weaker than the right because it is drilled
for the speedometer cable. To strengthen this component follow
directions in text and drawing. If the speedometer must be retained, use Porsche spindles as discussed in the text.

Front spindles can be given added strength by heliarcing spacer
to each spindle. Do not gas weld: keep the heat down. Never
straighten and reuse a VW spindle unless you prefer a tricycle.

Although at first glance this would appear to be trouble looking
for a place to happen, this is what the typical sand set-up looks
like. Bald tire and no shocks can be bad news anywhere except in
the sand. However, this fellow should have gone farther and
removed the brake drums, leaving only hubs to mount the wheel
onto the bearing. If no brakes are used on the front, get rid of
the drums.

Sturdy tubing welded to torsion tube protects steering box. Better protection would be had by a full-width skid plate curved up to join the massive bumper. Lights are protected by tape and cardboard when not in use.

welding the inner spindle spacer to the spindle. This spacer has been eliminated from the late front end. For those contemplating taking a Type III or Variant front suspension off the road, there is a heavy-duty spindle available. The left spindle is P/N 311 405 311 C; the right spindle bears P/N 312 405 312 C. These spindles must be used with seal 311 405 641 B and inner bearing 311 405 625 A. The outer bearing is P/N 311 405 645 A. No machine work is involved in swapping parts, though you should have access to a VW technical manual and a hydraulic bench press.

Frequent inspection and periodic replacement of the ball joints in the late suspension will provide trouble-free motoring off the road.

There is no particular advantage to running the Variant disc brakes off the road. For practical purposes they weigh as much as the drum assembly, and VW-based cars running off the road usually tend to lock up the front wheels first anyway. So more braking power is not needed. For highway driving and slalom events, their resistance to fade is worth the effort and money, but off the road this is just not the case.

Some off-roaders (and street buggists, too) use the larger 9-3/4" brake drums from a VW Variant (fastback, squareback or notchback) at the rear and keep the sedan-type 9-1/4 inch brakes at the front to obtain a differential in the braking action. This produces braking which is especially well suited to the high rear weight bias of the average buggy or sedan.

As an additional comment on the above, there are several dune-buggy-accessory manufacturers selling a switch or cutoff device to eliminate the front brakes for cars running off the road. By turning a lever or flipping an electrically-actuated switch, the hydraulic pressure is cut off from the front brakes. An increasing number of competitors are turning to this device because, in most cases, its use aids control of the vehicle while under severe braking conditions. By no means should this be considered necessary for the occasional and casual drive off the road. Neither should this be confused with the steering brake.

Baja runner's good ideas include an oversize washer to keep the shock in place if the rubber mount fails. Roll cage is braced to top of shock mount. Wiring is covered with plastic fuel hose and tied in place with nylon wire ties. Lights need protection.

Quick steering on buggies and sedans is proving to be a definite asset. Initial thoughts were that the increased steering effort would soon prove tiring. Reports from off-road racers indicate that the quick steering may even help to compensate (at times) to the slow reactions which are caused by fatigue. Crown Manufacturing developed a quick steering adapter (already widely copied) for the VW. It reduces steering from 2-7/8 to 1-7/8 turns lock-to-lock. This is the only quick-steer adapter that works with all VW's through '69.

Crown Select-A-Drop allows varying vehicle front height, an especially useful feature for dual-purpose buggies and sedans which see some street or slalom use.

VW sedan in the starting impound area at Ensenada. Prior to start of 1969 Baja 1000.

Rear Suspension

Rear wheels should be positively cambered for off-road use, especially at the start of a tough event. They'll sag into a neutral or negative camber with hard running, thereby reducing ground clearance.

Below: Torsion bar and trailing-arm serrations should be identified as to original position before separating the two. Scribe a line across the bar and plate serrations. "R" indicates a right-side torsion bar.
Bottom: Torsion arm slots permit varying axle location to adjust rear toe. Mark stock location of axle tube relative to plate before disassembly.

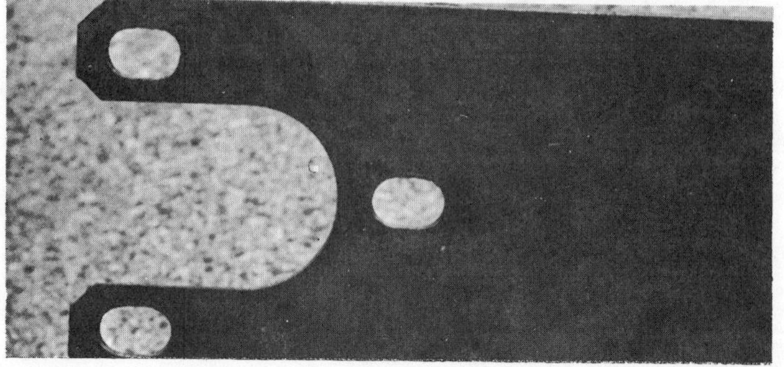

In many ways, the rear suspension of a VW-based vehicle is like the front: hard to beat. But one of the chores you must face sooner or later is that of changing rear camber. Due to the adjustment method, camber may be changed either a lot or a little. The amount of camber or decamber which should be applied in an off-road vehicle varies greatly. It is dictated by: loaded vehicle weight, tire size and wheel offset, terrain, whether the vehicle is to be driven at speed, and driver preference for a "certain feel."

We'll encourage you to do your own experimentation and just say that, normally, a lightened sedan and an even lighter glass-bodied car needs decambering to maintain the desirable handling trait of steering with the front of the car and having the rear follow!

Now for the bad news! A deplorable situation exists with any swing-axle suspension. Decambering the suspension for good handling inevitably results in destruction of the car before a rigorous race is completed. So, most racers compromise, and some will even settle for outrageously bad handling (positive camber) to ensure longevity of the car. There is no other choice.

Seasoned off-road competitors "crank in" a great deal of pre-load when setting up the front and rear torsion-bar suspensions. Their reason is to stiffen the spring rate so that the suspension never bottoms. If the suspension does not bottom, then things don't break. Additional spring rate can also be "cranked in" through the use of spring-over-shock assemblies, air shocks, or air bags. This does mean that you start the race with positive camber and worse handling than you would prefer, but it also means that you will probably be able to finish the race. It should be noted that torsion bars do sag as a result of off-road pounding, so a car which starts the "Baja 1000" race with positive camber will be decambered by the end of the race--from hard use.

Just for review, let's reconsider "camber." This is the angle at which wheels meet the ground, as viewed from the front or rear of the vehicle. Positive camber means the wheels point out at the top. Negative camber means the wheels point in at the top. At zero camber, both wheels are perpendicular to the road surface.

Stock Volkswagens are set with slight positive camber (the amount varies) so that the loaded vehicle does not constantly bottom out the suspension because of limited wheel travel. The more negative the camber angle, the less wheel clearance and upward axle travel which is available.

Volks' rear end is sprung by two solid-steel torsion bars housed in a large-diameter steel tube across the chassis. Both ends of the torsion bars are splined: the inner end fits into a splined

socket inside the housing and the outer end fits
the splined hub of the radius arm. The inner
splines contain 40 grooves and there are 44 outer
splines.

Advancing the inner-spline position one groove
rotates the torsion bar nine degrees. Moving the
outer spline a notch corresponds to eight degrees,
ten minutes. Thus, the bars can be adjusted in
5/6-degree camber increments in either direction.

Camber adjustment: Remove four 10mm nuts
holding both brake cables to the hand lever and
allow threaded cable ends to drop from their
holes. Cable housings may then be pulled from
their holes at the rear of the chassis tunnel to
obtain the necessary slack.

Disconnect the shock absorbers from either their
top or bottom mount. Before unbolting the half-
axles from the radius arms it is important to
indicate the original relationship of the axle to
the radius arm. The bolt holes provided in the
radius arm are elongated to permit the half-axles
to slide horizontally for adjustment of toe-in/toe-
out. Assuming that you are working with a
straight (unbent) chassis, mark the original position before unbolting the half-axles from the
radius arms. There is a groove in the axle
bearing housing above the upper rear-axle
mounting bolt. Mark the position of this groove
by striking a mark in the top of the radius arm
with a chisel or scribe. Thus, the original relationship of the arm and axle can be identified
later.

Approximately five minutes (1/12 degree) of rear
wheel toe-out is adjusted at the factory on new
and empty vehicles. Because of the placement
of the pivot points on the rear suspension, toe-
out increases slightly as the wheel moves toward
zero camber, and then decreases slightly as it
moves toward negative camber. If negative camber is desired, it is not necessary to change the
toe adjustment from stock location unless an
extreme degree of negative camber is induced.
If the rear wheels are set at zero camber, it may
be desirable to reduce the amount of toe-out
somewhat for better tire wear and less rolling
resistance. Amazingly close alignment can be
achieved on a flat floor if you have a big square,
string and a tape measure.

Moving the axle forward in the torsion arm slot a
distance of one millimeter reduces the toe-out
approximately eight minutes. The "shade-tree
mechanics" method of modifying toe is best
accomplished by striking a vertical line into the
radius arm directly in line with the front of the
bearing housing. After the axle has been unbolted from the radius arm, another line can be
placed 1mm or 0.5mm in front of the first mark
to locate the new position from the axle. By
making all markings clearly and locating them

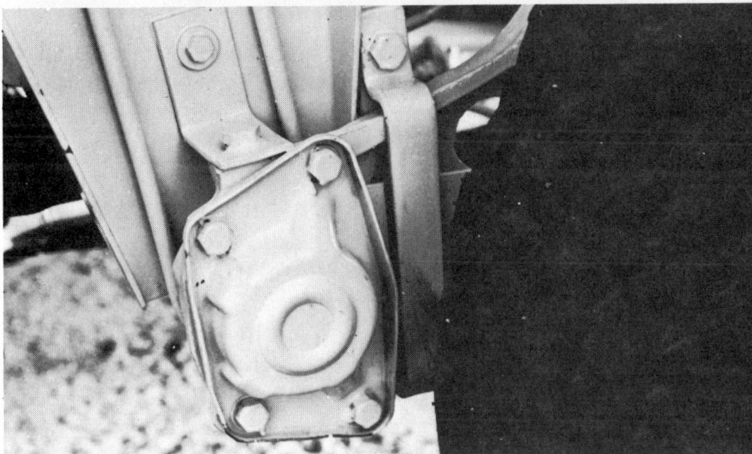

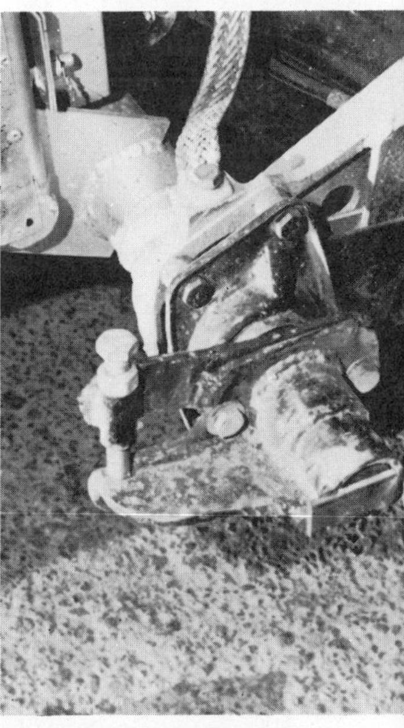

Low-cost insurance policy for VW rear-suspension pieces is a
strap welded or bolted (best) across the end of the torsion tube
housing to retain the torsion arm when the bottom stop beats
down. When this happens, shock absorbers pull apart and half-
axle swivel joints start chewing into the side retainer plates. Set
the torsion bars where you plan to run them before welding on
straps.

Right photo (above) shows Baja competitors' external adjustment
mechanism, retaining strap and *double trailing arm!*

accurately, chances for trouble in doing this job are slight.

With the original axle position marked, remove the three bolts holding the half-axle to the radius arm. With these bolts out, the axle can be pulled to the rear, leaving the radius arm (trailing arm) resting against the stop cast into the torsion-tube end piece. Remove four bolts holding the radius-arm hub-retainer plate. Pull off the cover plate and the outer bushing which is then exposed. See additional details on cover plates on the next page.

With a couple of large screwdrivers, pry the radius arm outward until it slips over the lower stop and drops to its lowest "no-load" position. Don't get in the way of the arm as it comes off of the stop, because you are actually unloading a giant spring which can hurt you considerably. Scribe a line along the top of the torsion arm so that the scribed line will be visible on the casting. You will use this as a reference to make quick checks of your progress as you adjust the torsion bars. Now mark the relationship of the radius arm to the torsion bar. Torsion bars for the left side (driver's side) of the car are marked on the end with the letter "L"; those for the right have an "R." This warns against installation on the wrong side of the car, which would cause loading in the opposite direction to that previously experienced and seriously weaken them.

Make a deep line with a chisel in the radius arm hub so that it is directly in line with one leg of the R or L. This permanently marks the original location of the splines. The radius arm may now be pulled all the way off the torsion bar end and repositioned to produce the desired degree of reduced camber. Moving the outer spline one groove is the usual method of decambering a stock VW for highway running. For buggies and stripped sedans, decambering two notches on the outer spline is plenty (16 degrees, 20 minutes), especially if you are using large tires. Any tire extending farther out than stock causes decamber. This is quite often too much decamber for serious off-road use. Increasing the camber (lowering the radius arm) five notches on the inner spline and decreasing the camber four notches on the outer spline will give a final 12-degree, 20-minute change from the stock setting.

The plan when making camber change is to make big positive camber changes on the inner spline and then reduce them with negative camber changes on the outer spline. Remember, one notch on the inner spline equals nine degrees of rotation, while one notch on the outer spline equals eight degrees, ten minutes. Increasing the camber one notch on the inner spline and decreasing it one notch on the outer therefore decambers the radius arm 50 minutes, or 5/6 of one degree. Though this fine an adjustment is

not necessarily needed to set up a vehicle for off-road use, it comes in handy when trying to improve the handling by making subtle changes in suspension and tire pressure. As you come close to the point you are trying to reach, you may find that the camber suddenly "jumps" 'way past what you wanted. Should that occur, turn the bar so that the inner splines are rotated 180° (half-turn) and start over.

It is most important that both sides be decambered exactly the same amount. After decambering, but before remounting the axles to the arms, measure from the lower edge of the bottom radius arm stop to the lower edge of the arm and make sure that both radius arms are depressed to the same degree. If not, change one of the adjustments to make the decamber as nearly equal as possible. With calibration completed, pull the radius arms upward until they rest on their lower stops. Coat the rubber bushings ("doughnuts") and radius arm hubs with graphite and lube the splines with white grease. Then bolt on the hub-retainer plate.

Bolt the half-axles onto the radius arms with careful attention to the reference marks mentioned earlier. Bolt the shock absorber back onto the mount, replace and adjust the handbrake cables, and the job is finished.

For the novice unfamiliar with the VW rear suspension, adjusting both sides may take an afternoon. After performing the task several times, gaining confidence, and rounding up the correct tools before setting to work, most long-time off-roaders can make camber adjustments in 30 minutes or less. VW manuals explain how to decamber with the halp of a special degree plate which fits onto the torsion arms.

If a vehicle is to be subjected to severe pounding off the road, such as that induced by racing, the chances are good that eventually the torsion arm's lower edge will bottom against the cast stop so often and so hard that the stop will be beaten down and inward. When this happens, shocks become the travel limiters and subsequently pull apart. Then the torsion arms bend and the instantaneous unloading of the torsion bar throws the vehicle into a severe positive camber attitude, usually on only one wheel. Needless to say, if this occurs at speed and possibly while the car is being turned, then you might spend some time picking burrs from your bonnet, or worse! There is a simple remedy: weld a piece of flat strap from the stop to the top of the torsion tube housing immediately above the stop. This prevents the plate from jumping over and down past the stop. Of course, this strap must be cut or broken loose each time the camber is adjusted. This strap (one for each side) should be considered as an essential item when setting up either a buggy, sedan, or truck for off-road.

Angle-iron tabs can be welded to the top and bottom of the torsion-tube housings, then drilled and threaded to permit bolting on this strap if you desire. This is neater and more practical than welding over the long run because the straps will have to be removed and replaced to get the rear suspension precisely as you like it. It should also be noted at this point that there are at least three torsion bars which can be used in VW's. These vary from 25mm (one inch) to 21mm (13/16") diameter, with the thicker bars from earlier sedans providing stiffer suspension and the most resistance against bottoming under severe loading conditions, especially for sedans. Two-piece torsion-bar cover plates on pre-'60 models should be welded all around because they are only spot welded. Or, replace them with one-piece plates (B-model Porsches) P/N 644.333.-151.000.

On most models the bottoming of the rear suspension (upward travel limit) is handled by a large rubber bumper attached to the upper rear of the torsion arm. Check this bumper frequently to see that it is in place and has not been broken off by the constant pounding. Any VW agency carries a large stock of these bumpers. Price is about fifty cents each. Carry spares!

The choice of shock absorbers for the rear of a VW-based off-road car is always good for an argument. Some enthusiasts get so involved with attempting to come up with something special that they overlook the function of the component, which is to absorb shock or to limit and absorb the oscillations of the spring (torsion bar). A weak shock-absorber arrangement allows the rear end to pitch forward severely and gives a spongy-feeling ride which is difficult to control at any speed. Too hard a shock will not allow the spring (torsion bar) to work or move throughout its design range. The ride is extremely rough because there is very little give when the entire weight of the vehicle leaves the ground and settles again, mainly on the rear wheels.

As on the front suspension, an adjustable shock such as those made by Koni or Armstrong for the Porsche work quite well. Some enthusiasts have had some success with coil-wrapped shocks (overload units). There is nothing wrong with this thinking if the spring is to be used somewhat as a progressive-rate spring would be used, that is, the coil goes to work just before the torsion arm reaches the end of its travel. In all too many cases, coil-wrapped shocks are taken from the box, bolted on, and the car run without any determination as to whether the coils will bind before the torsion bar completes its full travel. When coil bind occurs, suspension travel stops and you may as well have a solid piece of steel there! Breakage is the usual result.

Several firms produce coil wrapped shocks which can be used to augment rear torsion bar suspension. In the foreground is the fully adjustable Koni. Spring tension is adjusted with the dual rings threaded to the shock body. The other shock is an Armstrong. Both use large rubber bushings on the shaft to absorb bottoming shocks. This cushioning idea could be applied to other shocks with a minimum of effort.

GM's Delco Division makes a shock with an "air lift" built in. It can be run on the street with little or no air, and then pumped up for the rough stuff. They can be used to increase the spring rate so that bottoming does not occur. Bottoming breaks things.

Two areas have received almost no experimentation by dune runners. One is using air bags for bottoming devices and the other is adapting the new VW crossover compensating spring to the earlier vehicles. First the air bags: these are used with success and frequency on heavier forms of off-road equipment, but apparently have been overlooked by the lightweight crowd because nothing was readily available in kit form. By way of introduction, the air bag is a small, tough, inflatable rubber tube which can be pressurized after being placed inside a coil spring. As the spring compresses due to vertical suspension travel, the air bag is also compressed and gets harder (higher pressure internally) as the load increases. Thus, in this sense it is progressive, and if properly located along the half-axle shaft and set up so that it only "works" during the last two inches or so of wheel travel, the air bag could serve to prolong the life of suspension components by softening the bottoming shock.

Beginning with the 1967 models, a torsion-bar-type compensator spring was fitted to the stock VW rear suspension. This spring runs crosswise above the rear axle tubes and connects to the rear axle tube with a rod at each side. Functionally, this spring is an overload device to prevent excessive rear-wheel-camber variation when the vehicle is heavily loaded. The action of this rear spring or bar should not be confused with the anti-roll bar stabilizer at the front of the car. The action is just the opposite. Thus the rear bar is often called an "anti" stabilizer, which is not correct.

The spring allows an increased load-carrying
capacity for the rear suspension without using a
stiffer torsion bar. Because the spring is attached to the rear suspension, it only works
when both rear wheels move closer to the body.
It merely goes along for the ride when one wheel
is moving up and the other down. The point at
which the spring comes into action can be adjusted by adding or subtracting rubber bumpers
to make the spring work sooner or later, re-
spectively.

When the vehicle is lightly loaded, the spring
does not function because the buffers (at either
end of the spring) do not contact the stops on the
axle tubes. Only when the vehicle is loaded and
the buffers come into contact with the stops does
the spring begin to assist the main suspension
system. Because the overload spring mounts
are rigidly attached to the sedan body, the attachment of this spring on a buggy may pose
some problems. The springs are on all 1967 and
later VW sedans, squarebacks and fastbacks, as
well as on earlier square, fast, and notch-back
VW's.

Camber on most off-road vehicles gets checked
at the wrongest-possible time — while the car is
in the shop being prepared for a race. Torsion
bars — like any other spring — sag under a load.
The only correct time to check camber is when
you have fully loaded the car with the complete
complement of equipment which you'll be carrying
for racing or camping.

When front brakes are not used, lighten the drums as this owner
has done.

Top: Crown TranSupport includes large strap around both top
and bottom of the transaxle case to keep transaxle from moving
up and down. Shift tube easily shifts into neutral if transaxle
moves vertically. Fitting routes axle lube to a pump and through
a cooler for an off-road racer.

Bottom: Another view of Crown's TranSupport. Lower piece is
shaped to clamp around underside of transaxle-support yoke.
See page 21 for additional details.

The off-road enthusiast reader of this book is primarily concerned with the four-speed transaxles used in the "bug" or VW Type I sedan, the Variant and the several versions of the VW truck (transporter). There are two different swing-axle transaxles. Prior to 1961, the transaxle case was split, much like the engine case. Beginning with 1961, the main case is a single casting. This transaxle is referred to as the "tunnel-type."

Thus, you can quickly identify the transaxles by looking at them. If you spot one with four universal joints (one at each wheel and one at each side of the transaxle)--that's either a '68 Auto Stick Shift or a '69 or later model. These are discussed later in this chapter, and they do have the desirable synchromesh first gear. However, installation into an early floor pan requires welding on a bracket at each side.

The main disadvantage of the pre-'61 split case is not the case itself, but the small pinion bearing. An additional disadvantage is the weaker, non-synchromesh straight-cut first gear. Because of this non-synchro gear, you should stop the car to engage first gear. Of, if you are adventurous or rich, you can jam it in while the car is still rolling and take a chance that the gear won't break as you force it into mesh while the main-shaft is still turning. You don't want a non-synchro first gear for off-road use! Avoid this transaxle.

The split-case non-synchro-first transaxle uses identical mounts for the torsion arms, fork mounts and clutch cable, but has a front nose mount which differs from the later units. There are two ways to install the later transaxle into a 1960 or older chassis. The easiest way is to buy the following parts from the VW store, scooping them out of the 1960-67 bus parts bins: front transmission cover P/N 211 301 205H, gasket 211 302 215, shift rod 113 311 541 and transmission front mount pad 211 301 265 A. These bolt right into the early chassis. But, if you happen to have a '60 chassis, the mounting on the torsion tube has smaller bolts and the mount can be bushed to fit snugly with bushings from a transporter exhaust clamp/support, P/N 211 251 247. Don't try to get by with a sedan shift rod because it will not work correctly. Because the bus shift rod has its locator dimple or detent on the bottom, you'll have to drill a detent in the top of the shift rod to permit attaching the coupling from the chassis shift rod. An old coupler can be carefully set up in a drill press and drilled straight through from the original set-screw hole. Then attach the coupler to the bus shifter rod with the set screw and use a transfer punch in the new hole to locate a new detent in the top of the shift rod.

Transaxles, Gearing & Tires

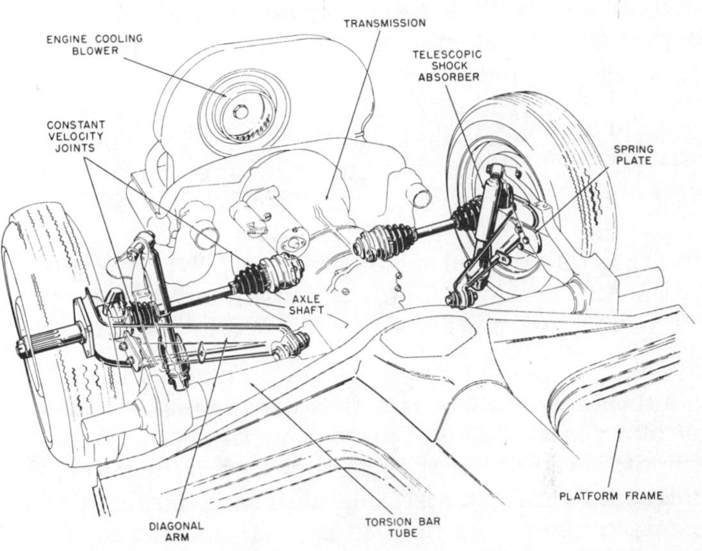

1969-70 VW rear suspension provides soft ride with improved roadability. Design keeps independently sprung rear wheels nearly vertical under any load condition. Each half axle has two constant-velocity U-joints. Overload spring is not shown in this AUTOMOTIVE INDUSTRIES drawing.

The second, but harder way to go is to use a new front mount on the torsion tube. These mounts are P/N 111 701 073C. Cut the old mount from the torsion tube with a torch. Position the new transaxle in the platform as it will normally be mounted. With the new mount in place on the nose of the transaxle, mark where the new mount should be on the back of the torsion tube. Remove the transaxle and weld the mount in place. While you're all doubled up under the rear end of the vehicle with all your welding gear out, weld a strap from the upper rear edge of the new mount to the top of the torsion tube. Reinforcing the bottom of the mount in the same manner is also a prudent idea.

We don't advocate that any novice tear into a VW transaxle unless he is intelligent, has a VW service manual and access to tools such as a hydraulic press, because service to this component takes experience and some special tools not found in everyone's shade tree garage. A lot of Joe Greasythumbs can take one apart and put it back together--but the trick is to put it back with all clearances and pre-loading "on the money." This insures long and troublefree service.

There are a couple of items that anyone can check, though, in an effort to ascertain if the transaxle you are about to purchase is worth anywhere near the amount of money being asked. If the transaxle is in a vehicle that can be driven-- drive it. A transaxle which jumps out of gear on acceleration or deceleration may have a broken front or rear transaxle mount or loose mounting bolts. Another possible cause is incorrect alignment of the shifting forks or a problem in the shift linkage. Badly worn gears are the next most likely cause. Does the gearbox grate, thump or howl in any gear? Don't worry much about reverse because this gear always "sounds different" from the four forward-speed gears. Any noise or combination thereof from a gearbox tells you that "something ain't right in there" and this could even mean that NOTHING is right in there. Beware of noisy transaxles because the fixin' cost can be a fierce $200 to $300.

"Broken-washer" syndrome is common and if caught early means only that the transaxle must be disassembled, and broken parts replaced. Symptoms are that it is almost impossible to shift into gear, sometimes shifter is jammed between two gears (locked up). If neutral is found after much searching, the car may still move ahead because the entire gear stack is adrift and causing strange things to occur. It's o.k. to drive home--if home is close by--but do not put off making this repair.

If the transaxle is out of the vehicle, block it up and drain the lube into a shallow pan. Expect grit and some small particles to come out, but if you begin seeing parts of gear teeth and what might have been a ball bearing at one time, you may get some idea as to why the transaxle is no longer in service.

While the transaxle is blocked up and the lube is draining out, turn the mainshaft. Do the axles turn? Use pliers to move the shifter shaft (sticks out of the transaxle's front). Shift into each of the gears and attempt to turn the mainshaft for each one. The axles should turn. If one simply refuses to turn, check to see whether the axle or backing plate on that side is bent. If the drum will turn freely, then the ailment is within the case. If you are still interested, you should inquire as to the local going price for replacing a set of spider gears because that is a rather common ailment.

If a transaxle is torn down, for any reason, it is well worth the time and effort to carefully inspect all bearings, gears and thrust washers and replace as needed rather than attempt to "get by" for another year or so with some worn component

grinding and grating away in the case and inflicting damage to other parts. Also, if the case is opened, there are several non-stock components (discussed in the following paragraphs) which may be added by those who want added "insurance" and increased performance. You should always replace the seals and the rubber boots when rebuilding a transaxle.

Most performance VW agencies and speed shops stock a limited-slip differential to replace the stock item which is not limited-slip. The advantages of this unit are readily apparent to anyone who has been stuck--and found that only one wheel was spinning and that the other was just sitting there waiting for the companion wheel to unstick itself. If you should be so unfortunate as to break an axle while tooling through the tulies, a limited-slip differential will allow you to continue with only one axle.

The limited-slip proves itself in slalom, drag-race and track competition. The unit is quite streetable and troublefree. They are available for either six- or eight-bolt ring gears. Make sure which you have before buying the limited-slip. The over-$200 cost of the unit is a major drawback. Some off-roaders don't like limited slips because these cannot be used with steering brakes.

Spider-gear breakage in VW transaxles is not at all uncommon in off-road applications. This is usually due to the severe (heavy) loads suddenly imposed on a gear when the vehicle lands on one

The ZF limited-slip assembly for the VW. Installation should be performed by someone completely familiar with the VW transaxle.

rear wheel while accelerating in a hard, non-giving type of terrain. Crown Manufacturing in Newport Beach, California makes "Beef-A-Diff" which doubles the number of spider gears and thus the load-bearing area in the differential carrier. The Beef-A-Diff cannot be used with the limited-slip differential previously mentioned, but in many off-road situations this unit is even more desirable than the limited-slip because it does not add to the already severe over-steer characteristics of most rear-engined buggies or sedans.

As is usually the case, there's still another method of strengthening the spider-gear portion of the transaxle. Gene Berg of Gene Berg Enterprises in Orange, Calif. reduces the spider-gear mortality rate by shim-preloading the large side gears against the spider gears so that the snap ring no longer flexes to allow the side gears to move away from the smaller gears under load. Berg uses 36HP VW crankshaft shims between the thrust plate and the thrust surface of the side gears. When correctly shimmed, there will be no spider-gear backlash.

We'd recommend both fixes in combination to make your transaxle as nearly "bullet-proof" as possible.

As part of their kit to adapt Corvair engines to the VW transaxles, Crown Manufacturing manufactures a thrust washer and spacer kit to be used between third and fourth gear on the pinion shaft of the tunnel-type transaxle. The two concave washers are made of beryllium copper to overcome the tendency to break in two--which is very common with the stock thrust washers when the extra power of the Corvair turns the VW transaxle. These tougher-than-stock thrust washers are a good investment for any transaxle subjected to harder-than-average usage--even with a VW engine. This kit can be used only in the 1966 and earlier tunnel-type transaxles.

Another fix which can be used to strengthen the thrust washer is to use the original 4th gear thrust washer P/N 113 309 361 which is about 0.100" thicker than the stock concave washer. The inside diameter must be ground out to fit and the sleeve between the gears must then be machined off so that only 0.002 to 0.003 inch clearance remains. This will cure the frequent problem of the transmission "jumping out of second." This is the spacer that goes on top of third gear before the sleeve goes on.

Despite the obvious advantage of running the all-synchro, tunnel-type transaxle, there are still a great number of highly serviceable split-case transaxles around. For non-competitive use off the road, the low-cost split-case transaxle can be put to good use if at least one modification is

Crown Manufacturing's Beef-A-Diff Kit adds two more spider gears to the VW transaxle to make a total of four, thereby doubling the load-bearing area on spider gears in the differential.

performed, as described below, in addition to making a regular habit of stopping before shifting into low.

Located between third and fourth gear on the main drive shaft is a split spacer sleeve. The split should be welded and both sides of the weld dressed down. Of course, when reassembling the gear box, all the bearings, synchro rings and gears should be checked for wear and replaced as needed. Welding up the sleeve split prevents the sleeve from being forced open and the gears from sliding together--but naturally this modification does not prevent other ailments which might be encountered because of normal wear and subsequent failure of other gearbox components.

The transmission supports and straps made by Crown Manufacturing provide good support with some cushioning effect. The transmission strap is P/N 5034 for all models. Transupport 5033-B is used in early chassis (through 1960) equipped with tunnel-type transaxle, and 5033-A is used in 1961 and later chassis with the tunnel-type transaxle. You should realize, of course, that any stiffening of the transaxle mounting will transmit more noise into the chassis. You'll have to live with the increased noise because the stock mounting is not adequate for any off-road use.

The installation of close-ratio gears is the remaining modification to the transaxle which involves the use of non-stock VW parts. Before discussing close-ratio gears and their advantages for street or off-road, one must first think of the rear tire as a gear.

The stock VW tire is approximately 25 inches in diameter. With this tire and a relatively stock engine, our vehicle will reach a top speed of 73 miles an hour on a dry, straight, level course with one occupant and no wind. Now, bolt on a set of tires measuring 30 inches in diameter. We do so to gain additional ground clearance for off-road running, and our vehicle now has about 2-1/2-inches more ground clearance (roughly half the increase in rolling diameter). Adding the larger tires changes our gear ratio. The final gear ratio (in any gear) is now effectively higher (lower numerically). We now have more of a top-speed situation--one which the hot rodder would term a "Bonneville gear." With tire-size increase, our car will now run 89 miles an hour under the same previous conditions (on paper!). But, the sad fact is that there is an excellent possibility that our vehicle won't even run as fast as it did with the stock tires. If it does, it may have to be driven in third gear instead of fourth. Additionally, we find that hills that were negotiated in third gear with stock tires now require dropping back to second gear with the 30-inch (ground clearance, remember) tires. By projecting these conditions still further, we might quickly reach the unpleasant and embarrassing situation of not being able to climb a hill in first gear because of the high final gearing created with the large-diameter tires.

Now let's take off the "tall" 30-inch tires which, on paper, will allow us 89 miles an hour. Bolt on some low-profile road-race tires with a rolling diameter of 20 inches. On paper, our top speed might figure out to be 59 miles an hour under the conditions previously set forth. Our sedan sits right on the ground, with no clearance for getting off into the rough--but, Boy!, can we climb hills, run at the drags and reach our top speed in a hurry!

These two situations illustrate what can happen when that final gear (the tire) is given little or no thought. The first situation (30-inch tire) is very common among buggy enthusiasts. It is quite evident on the dune buggies which are driven primarily or solely on the street. This is due to the fact that the larger tires (diameter and width) give a better appearance than the stock-size tires--which is usually the only reason for the change--but the enthusiast finds himself staying off the freeway most of the time because he simply can't keep up with the traffic... and he probably can't figure out why. Tire sizes as gear ratios just don't enter his thinking.

The small-displacement engine does not have enough power to pull the taller, wider tire effectively, thus the engine is always "lugging," or running in an rpm range where it can't develop its power. This usually leads to spending more and more on the engine in an effort to get per-

formance back up to that of a stock sedan. (If you are planning to spend money on your engine, be sure to buy our VW book before you start, as it tells you how to save money by avoiding useless parts and tricks that don't work.) When we speak of performance, we are including acceleration, because this aspect is greatly affected due to the change in final drive ratio through each gear.

Like much else in automotive design, gearing must be a compromise. We need adequate ground clearance, reasonable top speed, and enough twisting effort (torque) at the rear axle to move a wider-than-stock (for flotation as discussed in the tire information later in this chapter) tire over steep and often loose terrain.

First, determine how the vehicle will be used, what you expect from it and how much you are willing to compromise. For instance, let us assume you have a 40-horse sedan which is used only for off-road racing and, due to ground clearance requirements, must use a tall tire (not necessarily 30-inch, but taller than stock). If you plan on staying competitive, possibly going to a larger engine later on, and can run the vehicle at speed on a good percentage of the courses you race on, then the close-ratio gears will be a sound investment (about $75 each for third and fourth gear sets, not including installation). Only fourth is needed for most buggies ($69.50).

If this same sedan is to be used only for long weekend camping trips and enough driving to and from work to keep the battery charged, then you might decide that you don't need to install close-ratio gears. Plan on downshifting to third sooner and staying there longer. Don't think you'll be out of the running if you decide to race this combination in some of the longer events--you'll just be in third gear nearly all the time, while a similar car with close-ratio gears will be in fourth. Top speed of the two vehicles may be roughly the same, but the difference will show up in acceleration.

For drag racing and slalom courses, acceleration is much more critical. The "weekend Walter Mitty" who drives the car to work every day will usually install the close-ratio gears. He'll use stock tires on the street and switch to a short (smaller diameter) tire for drag racing.

A working knowledge of using tires as gears is invaluable if you want a top performing car. For those using VW transaxles, the following gear-ratio chart can be helpful only if used. Most speed shops sell a "dream wheel" or cardboard slide rule for quick computation of speed with a known tire diameter and final gear ratio at any rpm. Again, this is on paper. If the engine will not pull the final gear at the selected rpm, the calculations are worthless. For those in-

VW TRANSAXLE GEAR-RATIO TABLE		1200/1300 VW Sedan Six-bolt ring gear 4.375 ring/pinion	1500 VW Sedan Eight-bolt ring gear 4.125 ring/pinion	VW Bus & Truck 5.373 ring/pinion (including reduction)
1st gear	3.80	16.63	15.68	20.42
2nd gear	2.06	9.01	8.50	11.07
3rd gear				
close-ratio	1.49	6.52	6.15	8.01
close-ratio	1.38	6.04	5.70	7.41
1200-1300 (six-bolt ring gear) 61-66	1.32	5.78	5.45	7.09
68-69 bus	1.26	——	——	6.77
1500 Sedan & 63-67 bus	1.22	5.34	5.03	6.55
4th gear (see note)				
close-ratio	1.14	4.99	4.70	6.125
close-ratio	1.00	4.375	4.125	5.373
1200-1300	0.89	3.89	3.67	4.782
1500	0.82	3.59	3.38	4.41

NOTE: Ratios shown may vary, depending on how a particular transaxle was equipped. These ratios are all for the tunnel-type late 1200/1300/1500/1600 VW's. Early split-case 1100 and 1200's were equipped with 3.60 1st gear; 1.88 2nd gear; 1.22 3rd gear; and 0.79 4th gear. Split-case models have a non-synchromesh 1st gear. Special close-ratio 4th gear is required for VW's with splined pinion shafts: 68 IRS busses, sedans 118, 258, 723 and later, and Variants 318, 032, 600 and later. This gear is made by Crown Manufacturing.

clined to do their own "pencil pushing" the following formulas may be used by you, just as they are by racers the world over.

Rear gear ratios are just a matter of simple division. Divide the number of teeth on a driven gear by the number of teeth on the gear that is supplying the drive. For example, a ring gear having 37 teeth driven by a pinion gear having 9 teeth will yield a ratio of 4.11 to 1.

Going a bit beyond this, let's get back to that top-speed thing again. On the blackboard it looks like:

$$\text{Speed} = \frac{\text{engine rpm X loaded wheel radius}}{\text{rear axle ratio X 168}}$$

The way this equation is set up, the final figure will give speed in miles per hour if you put in loaded wheel radius as inches. Let's take an engine at 3000 rpm, a rear gear of 4.10 and a loaded tire radius of 14 inches. This combination shows up with a top speed of 61 miles per hour. Filled out, the equation above looks like:

$$\text{Speed} = \frac{(3000\,\text{rpm}) \text{ X } (14\,\text{inches})}{(168) \text{ X } (4.10)} = 61\,\text{MPH}$$

This is all very well if you have a tach (and you don't have a tach?). O.K., let's match up rpm to a known miles-per-hour figure. For this little chore, the equation becomes:

$$\text{RPM} = \frac{\text{speed in MPH X 168 X rear gear ratio}}{\text{loaded wheel radius in inches}}$$

Now then, we're back to the tall versus short tire--we never really left it! Naturally, as a tire's diameter gets larger, so does its circumference. This means that a taller tire covers more ground distance (linear travel) for every revolution than does a short tire. Thus:

$$\text{loaded wheel radius in inches} = $$

$$\frac{168 \text{ X rear gear ratio X MPH}}{\text{engine RPM}}$$

A word of caution before you start to "figger." To determine loaded wheel radius of any tire, inflate the tire to the pressure you plan to run, mount the tire on your car (or one of similar weight) and measure the radius (in inches) from the ground to the center of the axle shaft. Do not measure the horizontal radius of the loaded tire. On a low-pressure, high-flotation tire, the measurements will vary greatly between horizontal and vertical radius.

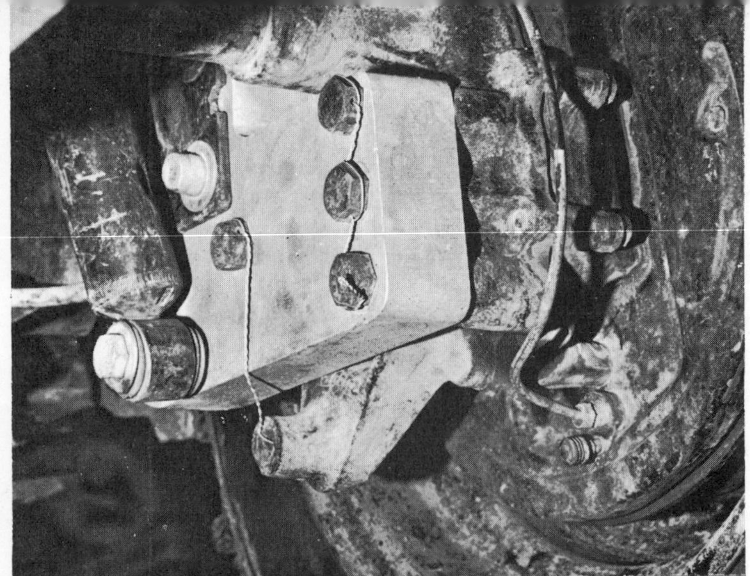

As noted in the text, truck transaxles use a reduction gear for lower gearing and more ground clearance. Unit may also be used in a sedan or glass-bodied car. Two shock-mounting methods are shown. One uses the stock mounting with bracing from the inside of the spacer plate, and the other (top photo) mounts the shock on the spacer plate. Any safety-wired capscrew is one less off-road worry. A 1¼″ to 1½″ thick aluminum or magnesium plate must be fabricated to use truck transaxle and reduction gears in a sedan or glass-bodied car with a sedan floor pan.

How to use the gearing chart: Don't try to make something out of the chart which is not there. This is simply a graphic means of letting you know where you are in regards to gearing with various VW gearboxes. For instance, if you have a 1500 CC sedan with an eight bolt ring gear, you know that the ring and pinion ratio is 4.125. If you are still with us at this point you can readily tell that the first gear is a 3.80, that second gear is 2.06 and that third gear is 1.22 (stock). This is where it gets to be fun. Running back up the column we find that we can install a close ratio third gear of 1.49 and tighten up the gap between third and second. The chart's value lies in giving a baseline from which "dream wheel" computations can be drawn in order to figure most effective tire diameter.

There's a real problem which occurs when you switch to the reduction-gear-type transaxle. Your car, whether buggy or sedan, will jump up at the back whenever you accelerate or shift, thereby sharply reducing traction when you need it. Watch a VW bus sometime and you'll get the picture. This hopping effect can be eliminated. Mount the axle housings so that they can rotate at the mounting point, rather than transmitting the torque reaction into the torsion arms. Keep the reduction-gear housing from twisting by attaching a drag link from the underside of the housing forward to the underside of the torsion tube. The drag links should be made from round tubing with Heim-joint ends. Adjustment of the mounting points so that the drag links are parallel with the torsion arm will produce a no-squat situation. Merely installing the drag links will not cure the jumping. The axle housings must be able to turn in their mountings at the torsion-arm ends.

By giving some thought to the gear situation and studying the list of possible combinations available, you may decide that the lower-geared bus or truck transaxles are just the ticket. Many off-roaders feel the same way because the swap to the bus units is an extremely popular one. The difference between sedan and bus/truck gear ratios is in the reduction gears at the end of the half axles, not inside the transaxle case (ring and pinion combinations are identical).

The only problem in installing the bus transaxle in a sedan is that of mating the half axles to the torsion arms because the bus half-axles have mounting points for the arm approximately 2-1/2-inches further outboard and about 2-1/2-inches lower. An aluminum spacer 1-1/4 to 1-1/2-inches thick must be fabricated and sandwiched between the half-axle mounting point and the torsion arm.

The sedan transaxle case may be retained and the bus half-axles used, but the torsion-arm spacer must still be used and, in addition, the ring gear must be reversed in the sedan case when the bus half-axles are used. Failure to do this will provide four reverse gears and one forward speed. Though top speed may be slightly reduced by using the reduction gears, five additional inches of ground clearance are gained, together with enough gear to plow, pull stumps or climb trees (not really).

If the ring and pinion has to be replaced in a sedan transaxle being changed to a reduction-gear type, consider using a bus ring and pinion because it was designed to rotate in the opposite direction and the teeth are cut differently from the sedan models.

Any VW engine will bolt to the bus transaxle, but the early tunnel-case transaxles may require some cutting away around the flywheel to permit installing 1967 engines which have approximately 0. 2" larger flywheels. The starter-motor pinion and outboard shaft are different from earlier models, requiring a smaller starter shaft bushing in the transaxle housing.

There are several points of confusion when considering some of the very late VWs. First, the "new" suspension in the rear. This new suspension is quite desirable and highly usable in off-road machinery. The new layout retains the torsion-bar suspension common to the older VWs, but departs from the older type by utilizing a universal joint at each end of each axle. Thus it quickly picked up the common nomenclature of "four-joint rear end. " The outside end of each axle is located by a large, stamped steel arm which pivots vertically from a bracket located close to the nose of the transmission case on the torsion tube.

Because of the two universal joints per axle, the wheels are kept very close to the same camber setting as they move vertically. This eliminates the problem of having the loaded wheel (outside wheel) tuck under in a turn while the inside wheel lifts, which often leads to a VW sedan on its side. Control is far more predictable, and the ride smoother and far more controllable off the road. As with the swing-axle rear suspension units used off the road, care must be taken to prevent the suspension from bottoming steel against steel. Heavy-duty shocks (such as some Konis), with a rubber bushing around the upper end of the plunger shaft, are good insurance for trouble-free service from the four-joint rear end.

These four-joint rear ends are found under late Type I sedans (the bug), the Variant, and the bus. Four-joint rear ends are used with the stick-shift four-speed, the automatic stick shift and the fully automatic three-speed. The automatic stick shift should not be confused with the fully automatic transmission. The automatic

4-joint rear end installed in buggy for 1969 Baja 1000 Race. Because these allow the wheels to remain nearly vertical under all load conditions, the vehicle height can be adjusted to provide desired ground clearance without need for using positive camber with associated ill-handling effects.

stick shift is a three-speed manual transmission coupled to a fluid-filled torque converter. Its functioning is similar to that of the Dodge-DeSoto-Chrysler Fluid Drive of the late forties.

There's no clutch pedal in the car because the automatic clutch (located between the torque converter and the gear box) is actuated by vacuum supplied by the engine. Thus at a stop light, with the automatic stick shift the vehicle can be left in gear and held in place with the brake. The engine continues to run. The vehicle will pull away from the stop in any gear, but will not upshift automatically. This must be done manually by touching the gearshift lever to disengage the clutch by a solenoid actuating a vacuum-shift mechanism. Relatively constant vacuum is maintained in a tank. The arrangement is fine for little old ladies who are not in a hurry and don't plan to go off the road. But there is much to go wrong with this unit in a severe-use situation and it should be the last possible choice for an off-road transmission.

The fully automatic transmission is something else again. It's fully automatic with no clutch. Gear changing is effected with a console-mounted selector very similar to those found in American-produced vehicles. With the selector in third gear, the transmission automatically downshifts as vehicle speed falls. Thus, when moving from a stop in third gear, the transmission is in low gear. As vehicle speed increases, an automatic shift will occur to second gear and then so on into third gear. There is a parking gear, and reverse can only be engaged after the shift selector is pulled up and then moved into position. There are no vacuum lines or tanks. Power application is very smooth and a real aid to moving through loose terrain with a minimum of wasted motion and wheel spin.

All the fully automatic transmission vehicles also contain the four-joint rear suspension which requires welding on new pieces to put this assembly into an earlier chassis.

If the fully automatic transmission is used off the road, fluid should be changed quite often in an effort to flush out dirt before it has a chance to clog an orifice and thus cause the automatic "internal pains" which could prevent it going into gear or cause rapid wearing of the close tolerance valves. Despite the obvious advantage of smooth torque application to the ground and delivering a more refreshed driver to the destination, there is one disadvantage to an automatic (any automatic) being used off the road.

In a hard-start situation (dead battery, etc.), it is quite difficult to push any vehicle having an automatic fast enough in rough terrain to effect an easy start. But, if you always travel with another car, as recommended in the chapter on going off-road in safety, you could carry a set of jumper cables and eliminate most of that worry.

Speaking of hard starts, let's go back to tires. Quit mumbling; just because you're now thinking of the tire as a gear doesn't give you a license to become the Tire Expert in Residence. In taking a vehicle off the road, the tire-and-wheel combination must be thought of as a durable flotation and traction device.

By durable we mean that you must have enough faith in the tire and wheel combination that you would drive a VW sedan the length of Baja California without carrying a spare! We're not advocating that you do that--just that you develop that much faith in what you put on the ground.

The terms flotation and traction shouldn't confuse anyone. A "skinny" tire, as used on stock VWs, sinks right into soft silt or mud simply because the vehicle weight is concentrated on a very small "footprint." Triple the area of this footprint by going to a wider tire and the loading

per square inch is reduced naturally and the vehicle does not tend to sink. Thus it has flotation.

Traction is simply the tire's ability to grab onto the terrain to move the vehicle. Here tread pattern becomes important. A drag strip tire offers maximum traction with no tread by simply putting a very large amount of soft rubber onto the smooth asphalt. This is an extremely tractive situation. The same tire is worthless off the road for any size or weight vehicle--because the tire offers no grip to rock, sand or mud. All this may be like saying that snow is cold to most of you, but following a hard rain shower in the middle of Baja, we encountered a four-wheel-drive pickup shod with street-type cheater slicks. During the course of pulling the truck out of the muck, the driver said he got the tires because "they sure looked good." This should be your very first tip on how not to pick an off-road tire. What looks good on a chrome wheel in a tire shop might be the hot setup for the drive-in crowd, but will they be around to get you out of trouble?

The greatest attention, effort and money should be concentrated on the tires for the rear--the driving tires. They are far more critical than the combination strapped onto the front rims.

First, let's get to wheels. This is a sore subject. When this off-road thing really got rolling, a lot of guys figured they could make a buck by custom-building wheels. This is a relatively simple matter. A trip to a wrecking yard and a little work can yield 15-inch rims which are 8 inches wide: some large American cars such as Buick, Olds, Cadillac and Chrysler have rims 6-1/2 inches wide which can be reworked to 8 inches without having to resort to heavier truck rims. The center can be chiseled or cut from the 6-1/2-inch rim with a torch. Then a VW wheel center can be cut down (usually on a jury-rigged flame cutter), dropped into the rim and welded into place. Let's go back over that process. That wrecking-yard rim could have been tweaked or fatigued without showing it. Was any damage done when Clod Bighammer started working on those rivets with chisel or torch? Was the VW wheel center cut in a perfect circle as it was trimmed from the rim? Where did the VW wheel come from? Wrecking yard? What was it doing there? Bent rim? But the center looked O. K. ? Couple all of this up and then weld it together and you've got just the wheel to bang and bash around off the road. While you're sitting there squirming, let's go a little farther with this situation. Many enthusiasts wind up running something in the neighborhood of an eight-inch-wide rim in the rear of a VW-powered machine. The cheap way out (and we do mean cheap) is to punch the center from a rim (say six-inches wide), split the rim, weld in a section to give the additional width, then weld in the VW center section. Needless to say, alignment and strength are all fighting for a berth on this rim and many times neither one of these vital factors winds up riding with you.

While we are dissecting wheels, let's take a closer look at the center section of a wheel, that part which bolts to the drum. Notice that the center section of a stock wheel is curved; that when viewed from the edge, the center bulges outward from the relatively flat area that bolts to the drum. Then after this bulge, the center curves back to meet the rim. The reason for this is to get strength under side loading. We bring this up because several "custom" wheel centers are stamped from flat or slightly curved plate. Avoid such centers for off-road use because they have insufficient resistance to bending when subjected to side loading.

One of the problems encountered by the wheel-manufacturing companies is making a wheel round. This roundness is measured in terms of radial runout. Excessive radial runout causes a wheel to hop, reducing traction and steering control and putting dangerous stress on other suspension components. Radial runout at the rim should not exceed 0.035-inch (1/32-inch). A wheel with excessive lateral runout will wobble. Besides causing control loss at high speeds, a "wobbler" can cause premature failure of the wheel or vital suspension components. Lateral runout on the rim should not be more than 0.045-inch.

Now, of course, all these guys welding wheels together in their backyards are measuring all of this, right? And they're rejecting all those wheels that don't measure right up to snuff, right? Get serious. There are wheels being sold that wouldn't be safe on a hearse.

A competitor in a dune buggy in a recent Baja off-road race never made it off the pavement because the center of the wheel and the rim parted company as he slid into a turn. After picking himself and the wrecked car from out of the brush, our hapless race driver then discovered that the center and rim had never been welded together, they had just been forced together!

New, one-piece, eight-inch rims are available. So are new VW wheel centers. A number of firms import new wheel centers for this purpose. If a wider wheel is sought, look for a two-piece rim that has been made by cutting and welding two new one-piece rims so that there is only a single weld around the center. This is a much more acceptable method of construction than adding a band of steel between rim halves.

Lightweight aluminum wheels are spun from aluminum sheet by Chassis Engineering of San Diego. Chassis Engineering's wheels are two "pie-plate" assemblies which bolt together. 5.5-pound wheel shown here has the pie plates welded together. *Regardless of what kind of wheels you buy — whether steel, magnesium or aluminum — check for runout before you accept the wheels or mount the tires!*

Many off-road racers consider one-piece rims to be the only answer. Why? Because these can be bent very far out of shape and subsequently semi-straightened with a hammer to allow continuing in the race.

The term offset is often heard in discussions concerning wheels, and the term perhaps needs some clarification and explanation. Offset is the distance the rim is moved outward or inward from the wheel center. In other words, are the tires effectively moved in toward the centerline of the car or outward to give it a "widetrack" look? When the rim is moved outward (widetrack), the offset is called positive offset. Moving the rim inward is known as negative offset.

An offset wheel must sometimes be used to move large tires away from the inner body panels.

Rear-wheel opening on Variant was radiused — then filled with Gates XT Commando. Booster spring was added for racing.

Below: Despite repeated warnings from manufacturers and others, very wide racing tires continue to be used on the street. They have a minimum of sidewall protection, are most untractable on wet pavement and offer shaky road-holding ability on dry pavement as camber changes. These tires would be quickly destroyed in rocky off-road use.

This is especially true of rear tires on a VW sedan. However, the amount of positive offset should be kept to a minimum. Positively offset wheels change the leverage on the torsion bars so that the bars are effectively smaller. Thus, you might have to use larger-diameter bars from an early chassis and/or crank-in more pre-load into the torsion bars to get the spring rate sufficiently stiff so that the chassis won't bottom out. There is usually more clearance at the front (of any vehicle), so positively offset wheels are seldom necessary at the front. Even so, many automotive buffs insist on running positive-offset wheels in the front because "it looks neat." Maybe. The fact of the matter is that a positively offset wheel causes a fantastic increase in wheel-bearing loads. The result is constant replacement of those items. Although the danger of breaking a spindle on the street due to increased loads is small, the possibility of this on an off-road vehicle because of positively offset wheels in the front is pretty good. Even the Janowski spindle fix won't save you from the loadings inflicted by positive-offset rims.

Don't go overboard on size. Let's say you've got a sedan used for off-road camping trips. A 15" X 8" wheel is plenty for the back and a 15" X 6" is all that's needed for the front. Actually, you'd probably be ahead of the game by running stock VW wheels up front unless you plan to run through a lot of soft mud. If the VW wheel is retained in the front, start shopping for a VW snow and mud tire. Settle for nothing less than a full four-ply tire. Don't be confused with four-ply rating. This means that the cord size has been raised so that tensile and impact strength equals four cords. This never quite works out to your advantage off the road. Get full four-ply tires.

What about running Mag-type wheels off the road? Go ahead. There is no evidence to indicate that these wheels won't take the loading stresses handed out by off-roading. In fact, many of these wheels (various brands and sizes) have been used successfully by off-road race cars. They claim that less unsprung weight means less damage to the tire/wheel combination. Side-wall bulge for proper rim protection is a must. Those wheels with a steel rim and cast center can be straightened like a stock rim--with a hammer. When using wheels with cast rims, take it easy in the rock. For sand-dune or secondary-road applications, these wheels can be effectively used to reduce weight.

For the front tires you are seeking a tread pattern which will provide maximum lateral stability. In other words, you want a tire which will point the vehicle the way you are steering it. A rather open, radial tread is needed for this. Several large tire firms, Goodyear and Armstrong, just to name two, produce an implement tire with straight cuts for the tread. These have given excellent results in hard running off the road in varied terrain.

We've recommended sticking with the stock VW wheel in the front for most applications. There are two reasons for this. In the first place, this wheel is lighter than any other "made-up" steel wheel--and reducing weight for off-road running is a constant battle. Secondly, when a larger-than-stock tire is placed on the stock VW rim, the sidewall of the tire bulges out past the edge of the rim. Thus, when you slide into a rock, the tire gets there first--then the rim. Let the tire take the gaff. Bash the rim back into shape and go!

Around back you'll need something about ten-inches wide to get much of a bulge past the rim. Again, the use of snow and mud tires with a coarse, open-tread pattern is best. Because of the extra load around back you might shop for a six-ply-rated full four-ply--this is an indication of extra strength--but certainly should not be thought of as a mandatory requirement for a rear tire.

Keep in mind that as rim width increases, foot-print increases and rim protection decreases. If you are setting up a sedan or buggy for tra-versing the muddy Kansas wheat fields or one of the sand dune areas of the country, you can go to 10- or 12-inch rims and gain maximum flotation. For this application rim protection is not needed. In the Western part of the United States, desert running demands rim protection--the ground is generally harder and flotation less of a problem. Thus we go to an eight-, seven- or even six-inch rim for the rear. Keep in mind that a 30-inch diameter tire will tend to bog the engine; that a "super tread, super footprint" tire will also tend to pull an engine down--thus you can get to a "too much tire" situation rapidly, espec-ially with the VW engine--which never had too much torque anyway.

For the sand, it is difficult to go too wide on the rims. The wider the rim — the greater the flotation. Although wide rims are used to get stiffening for the sidewall of the tire in road rac-ing, observe the sand dragsters and you will note that they use the widest rims allowed by the rules. The tires used for sand have sidewalls which are flexible. When the tire, rim and inflation combo are "just right, " the tire "pooches" out at the sidewalls just above the ground contact area. Many buggy/sedan owners carry special low-pressure tire gages. And, they also look at the tire to see how it is "pooching. "

Although big-diameter tires look "boss" on the back, keep the gear ratios in mind. We've noted that many who compete in the longer off-road events have gone to smaller and smaller tires with each new race. Must be a reason!

An excellent example of tires and wheels fitting the job. Good-year Terra Tires at rear give flotation and traction. The sidewall bulges outward just past the rim edge for protection against a rock bending the lip inward. Front rims are reversed on stock VW centers and shod with Gates Commandos. This excellent tire for the front has an open radial-tread design which tends to clean itself so that it does not gum up with mud. Roll cage is braced fore and aft and the front shock mount is tied into the upper frame rail for added structural rigidity.

Tom Cepek's tire caliper measures 8.45–15 recapped Nylon tubeless at 27½″ diameter on an 8-inch rim for rock use, and 27″ on a 10-inch rim for sand operation. This popular tire has a 9-inch wide general purpose sand/rock tread pattern. Usually used with stock 5.60–15's or small Armstrong Norseman or implement tires on the front wheels.

Front and rear tires are not always so different, but this is a good racing and general-purpose combination which can be run on a vehicle when most of the weight is carried by the rear axle. Both are Goodyear tires. Straight-tread tire is basically a farm-implement tire which is good for sand and large tire is similar to Goodyear's Pikes Peak racing tire. It has a different cord structure and a hard compound rubber.

Armstrong Norseman combination for rocky off-road going: 29″ L78–15 rears and 26″ 6.95–14 fronts are largest mud/snow tires available. Rears mount on 8″ rims (bead-to-bead) for general purpose, 10″ for sand.

We mentioned earlier that one of several implement tires were excellent choices for the front of a VW-powered vehicle. They are--but they were not designed to run at speed on the pavement whereas the snow and mud tires are dual-purpose designs. The larger implement tires (11" X 14" or 15") for 9- to 12-inch rims are quite shaky at speed on the pavement. Because of weight (tire and rim will weigh about 70 pounds), the rotating mass must be balanced to the Nth degree or the wheels acquire a mind of their own about where they want to take the vehicle at about fifty miles an hour.

How about tire sealers or sealant materials? Until Aguirre Enterprises introduced their "Flat-Proof," experts claim that there was no sealant that could get the job done in an off-road application. This stuff seals both tube-type and tubeless tires. Holes caused by cactus spines, nails or even minor bead damage are sealed without loss of air. Static and dynamic balancing should be done first, according to Dick Cepek — then you can add the Flat Proof. The availability of a sealant that works, allows the tires to be balanced and is reasonably priced is starting a trend away from the use of inner liners — which are discussed on the following page.

You can draw some arguments on this, but experience has shown that tubeless tires work as well, run cooler and are as trouble-free as tube-type tires. In fact, tubeless tires carry the advantage of being able to flex severely and hold air whereas prolonged flexing (as in very-low-pressure applications) can cause a tube to pinch and chafe and thus lose air. However, should you bend the rim, there goes the air pressure, and unless you are a metal-bending expert, you may not be able to hammer the rim contour back into the bashed rim so that the tire will again hold air. Inflating a tubeless tire off-road may also be a bear of a problem.

On a dune buggy or gutted VW sedan, relatively low air pressures are best. Here again, terrain and vehicle weight have a great deal to do with this, but most all applications can be covered with less than 20 PSI. In the case of dune running, five to eight pounds pressure is not uncommon. Low pressure provides maximum flotation and tractive ability. There is one danger, or rather ill, that follows low pressure; that is spinning the rim within the tire due to a lack of gripping power of the bead against the rim. When this occurs, the stem is yanked from the tube and the tire goes flat. This can be cured by drilling the rim and bead with a 1/8-inch drill and using sheet-metal screws to secure the tire bead to the rim. Eight screws per side are sufficient. Don't forget to remove these screws before attempting to break the tire from the rim.

Stock VW snow tire (nearest camera) is only adequate for limited off-road running. These do not provide flotation as given by larger off-road tires, nor do they offer directional control in sandy going. Goodyear's implement tire is in the center. Behind that, Gates' snow and mud tire which is especially good off-road in rocky terrain. Gates is self-cleaning with adequate ribs to keep going straight.

Experiment with tire pressures. If you are running a sedan, start off with 20 PSI, then re-run the same terrain at 15 PSI. The idea is to let the sidewall flex and absorb as much of the shock as possible, but do not allow the side walls to wrinkle. When running over rock, go down with the pressure gradually and run easy. You don't want the rim to move down so far on loading that the sidewall will be cut by the rim. Try to "feel" how the tire is "working." This is a matter of experience and taste for a particular handling feel of a vehicle that comes with time. There is no quick way to teach or to learn this.

Tire inner liners gained a lot of acceptance for off-road use for lack of a good sealer. An inner liner is something like putting another tire inside a tire. An inner liner should not be confused with a tube, although they do hold air. The liner is much stiffer than a tube and is designed to carry quite high pressures. In drag racing, the inner liner pressure is often run up to 50 PSI or more to keep the tire bead forced onto the rim. This is not necessary--in fact should not be done--for off-the-road applications because this stiffens the sidewall of the tire. 25-30 PSI is about normal off the road for an inner liner for a lightweight vehicle. Because the air held in the inner liner is independent of that held in the tire (tubeless-type only), the liner is normally not affected if the tire is punctured. The tire sags to the inner liner (about an inch) and continues to run. You shouldn't make a practice of running long distances with this, but that is the purpose of the inner liner--to get you back to civilization without having to change or repair a tire.

Mounting an inner liner can be a real bag of snakes for the novice. Place the inner liner inside the tire, then pull both over the rim, then both down into the rim. Seat the tire on the lower edge of the rim first, then follow suit with the inner liner before attempting to squeeze both up to the upper edge of the rim.

There are a few things that you should understand before you ruin a tire off the road and attempt to make a guarantee stand up at the dealership on a Monday morning. Your chances of collecting on a ruined tire, or even getting some sort of adjustment toward the purchase of a new one are slim if the tire is listed as a truck

Inner liner (left) fits inside tubeless tire, inflates to a higher pressure than the tire itself to protect against damage from rocks and to aid in keeping extremely low-pressure tires on the rim. Liner also holds tire up when the tire is punctured. On a lightweight car this is a practically fool-proof combination. Once you have blown out a liner-equipped tire, stop racing until the tire is fixed. *Limit your speed or excessive heat will be generated by the liner rubbing against the casing.*

tire, unless the tire failure came as a direct result of poor workmanship or material--which seldom happens these days.

If the tire was sold as a passenger-car tire, and many snow and mud tires are, then your chances for an adjustment are somewhat better. The "sticky" point here is the dealer's decision as to whether the tire had been "abused" before it failed. This is because most tire companies have an "abuse clause." If the dealer decides that "abuse" was not involved, then an adjustment will normally be made on the basis of tread wear.

Does all of this sound too complicated? You're right--it is! The simple way out would have been for us to print the various tire companies' guarantees and let you figure it out. But, the guarantee interpretation varies considerably between dealers in these odd-ball situations involving tires which have obviously been run down the side of a mountain before final failure.

As of 1969-70 when this book was written, at least on the West Coast, the tire dealers who specialize in off-road tires were being quite liberal in interpreting the "road hazard" guarantee. Some were making adjustments on the amount of remaining tread wear, despite what a tire looked like — or what abuse it had obviously been subjected to. This may change with time, but meanwhile — a lot of off-road tires are being sold because of this liberal interpretation.

Check with other off-roaders in your area on where they purchase tires. Find out what kind of treatment they have gotten when they wound up taking one back. Ask several dealers what their policy is in this matter before you buy. Be honest with them. Tell them that you will be taking the tire off the road before you buy it and tell them where it's been when you bring it back. Most of them see more tires in a week than the average guy ever will, so don't think that you're going to trick them. No chance.

Again, let us caution against using a rear tire which cannot be effectively pulled by the engine. It is far better to use a smaller-size tire, sacrificing some flotation and tractive ability but remaining able to spin the tire, than it is to have more than adequate flotation and traction to the point that the slip comes at the clutch. Mark up a couple of points for the automatic in this department. Let us get back to a silt hill: You're running a 30-inch tire on a 40-horse sedan. Prior to attacking the hill, you had to ford a small stream. Doing this, you had to slow almost to a stop in order not to drown out the engine, but wound up with one plug shorted out anyway. You reason that you cannot sit in the creek and dry off the plug and that all you need to do is crest the hill--then you can dry it off. But a

three-cylinder engine pulling two fat guys and a sedan up a hill is liable not to make it with high-flotation, low-pressure tires--so the clutch begins to slip. You pour the coal to it. More slip. You're in low gear, so that takes care of that. What it boils down to at this point is whether the cylinder will pickup before the clutch burns out.

In this "sweaty-palms" situation, you'd be ahead of the game (and probably the hill) with a tire that would slip or spin somewhat and continue to "churn" up the hill.

With the stock VW rear-end ratios which are available, you cannot get the rear ratio low enough to allow the engine to work in the correct rpm range to supply enough torque to get the car over some obstacles--or up some slippery hills--without spinning the tires. Obviously, for the continuing good of the entire sport of off-roading, throwing dirt by spinning tires, and thereby gouging ruts into the landscape, should be avoided wherever possible. But, there will be some hills which can only be attacked with the wheel-spinning, dirt-throwing, rut-gouging approach--at least with a VW-powered off-road machine. The need for such tactics is reduced by using the transporter rear end and by using the smallest-diameter tires that you possibly can for the terrain to be covered.

If you install tires which are too large in diameter (anything greater than 30 inches begins to get you into a trouble area), you will be creating at least two problem areas. One of these is the inability of the engine to pull the car at highway speeds in fourth gear, and the other will be the inability of the engine to pull the car over obstacles at lower speeds. Big rubber will "bog" the engine, preventing it from working in the rpm range where good torque can be produced.

There is another point to throw into this gear-ratio/tire-diameter consideration, and that is the need for high speeds in fourth gear in some cross-country off-road races. The VW engine's tiny displacement will only haul your car just so fast with the optimum gearing, tire size, etc., for top speed. You may well be better off if you select a gear ratio/tire size that cuts the top speed to make the entire combination more driveable when you are picking your way carefully over rough terrain. The entire problem of getting the correct gear ratios has caused many off-roaders to use close ratio gears in the third and fourth slots of their transaxles, to increase the displacement of the VW engine by stroking and boring, as described in our VW book, and in some instances, to change over to Corvair power as detailed in our Corvair book. Bigger displacement (more cubic inches) is the only "vice-less" hotrodding technique. The full facts are in the other books.

Engine Preparation

Carefully prepared engine shows that owner has been off road on previous occasions. Note dual coils mounted off of engine, fuel filter, dust-proofed distributor, skid plate and remotely mounted centrifugal-type air cleaner. Chroming is an extravagance to avoid because it makes engine run hotter. Same is true for valve covers. Leave 'em rough and paint 'em black!

Perhaps conspicuous by its absence in this book is a discussion on how to turn the 40 horse VW engine into a 200-horsepower fire breather with drugstore parts on a Saturday afternoon. There are several reasons for that. In the first place, this simply cannot be done. The gutty little engine can be successfully modified to produce an astonishing amount of horsepower. This takes know-how, skill and time. We cannot tell you how to do this in one paragraph, or a page or a chapter--so we wrote another book to outline the step-by-step procedure for pulling horsepower and life from a Volkswagen engine for street, off-road or racing use.

The volume goes into great detail in explaining the procedures and pitfalls of hopping up the VW. Scores of dyno runs were logged as components were checked, modified and then rerun. Machining instructions, part numbers and horsepower-producing combinations are laid out with more than a hundred photos. Once into this book, you'll see why we simply can't do justice to the VW engine as a small part of one volume. That's why it's separately covered in "How to Hotrod VW Engines" by Bill Fisher.

And, there's still another book for you to consider if you plan to use a Corvair to power your off-road machine, "How to Hotrod Corvair Engines" by Bill Fisher.

What we will do in this book is attempt to outline some of the problems and cures in taking an engine off the road with special emphasis on the VW. We'll stand by a wicked pun and say that basically the problems are elementary--like water and dirt--and various combinations thereof.

More simply stated, the problem is in keeping these elements out of the engine. This is far easier said than done, yet with a little patience and thought an engine can be sealed quite tightly. Before starting to seal up an engine, first make sure it is clean. Use your own tricks here: steam, solvent, soap and water or whatever. Get it clean! No oil film, no flaking or chipped paint.

Now, remove every nut and bolt, preferably one or two at a time. Clean each one thoroughly, first with solvent and then with Loc-Quik. Then put a drop or two of Loctite thread-locking compound on the threads prior to reassembling and torquing the nuts or bolts into place. You can buy Loctite at bearing houses and at some automotive supply stores or parts houses.

With tape, hoseclamp, glue or a combination of all three, make a bag of polyurethane foam over the end of the breather tube which hangs down from the oil filler hole or route a piece of flex hose from this breather into the air cleaner.

Notice how the slot in the generator case is covered *but not closed* with tin to prevent dirt from falling in and yet allow cooling air to exit. Body putty and hose clamps seal dirt from carb/air cleaner junction.

RTV Silastic sealant on throttle linkage ends prevents dirt and dust from causing wear and premature failure. This excellent material can be used in a variety of ways on an off-road vehicle. Tubes of the sealant are available at large hardware stores, electronic supply houses, and marine dealers.

Polyurethane is the porous filter material used in late GM air cleaners. Pick up a used one from the local service station trash can. Cut a small section out, clean it in solvent and go to work on that vent. If other vents are installed on the engine--such as the valve covers (breathers are discussed in our VW and Corvair engine books), these vents should also be covered with polyurethane. Do not use foam rubber for this because some foams won't pass air--thus you have no vent, and engines must be vented. Also, some foam rubber will disintegrate in gasoline or oil. Other versions have larger holes than the polyurethane. After the polyurethane is in place, squirt several drops of engine oil over the exposed surface. Note bottom photo on page 93.

Polyurethane foam can be glued in place over or around all vented areas.

Place a bead of non-hardening putty (automotive "dum-dum") or Silastic RTV (liquid rubber) around the area where the carburetor mates with the air cleaner. We'll get to air cleaners later. There are several ways to "attack" the distributor but results are the same with any properly executed method. Inspect the cap for any cracks or nicks, especially on the edge which seats against the metal housing. If all's well with the cap, remove the rotor. Stretch a small piece of plastic sheeting (bread wrappers or "Baggies" work fine) across the top of the housing, pulling it tightly down against the leading lip that mates with the cap. Carefully cut a hole in the plastic so that the distributor shaft extends through. Install the rotor. At this point you can go one of two ways. Coat the seating edge of the cap with rubber or trim cement, shove it back into place and latch the hold-down clips. The other route is to simply shove the cap back in place, pop on the hold-down clips and run a bead of the putty or Silastic RTV around the outside edge of the mating surfaces.

With new wires and connectors shoved into the cap, press putty or Silastic around each wire where it enters the cap. When this is done correctly, you can run a steady stream of water from a garden hose on the distributor while the engine is running and it will never miss a beat.

The putty treatment is somewhat harder to apply to the spark plugs in an effort to waterproof and dustproof this end of the spark. 1969 VW spark plug connectors are said to be waterproof and perhaps they are. The others are close but still need to be sealed with trim cement or Silastic RTV--not rubber cement because of the heat.

Run a generous bead around the connector end where it pushes on to the plug insulator, then shove it into place and leave it there. Seal the top end of the connector where the wire passes through in the same manner. Now you'll have to

In an effort to keep the engine compartment as clean as possible, the owners of this sedan have used duct tape to seal the crack between engine and body sheet metal. Extra thick rubber molding was used around the deck lid to augment the tape seal.

Fram oil filter adapter kits for VW engines bolt into place with a minimum of effort and only hand tools are needed for the job. Cost of the entire filter kit is only $15. The incorrectly mounted coil will vibrate excessively and destroy the fan shroud.

be careful when pulling a plug because that rubber seal will have to be broken loose. Grip as low as possible, twist and pull slowly or you'll yank the connector from the insulator boot.

The previously described procedure will not produce a waterproof engine--that is, one which can be run underwater. The engine will run through streams deep enough to cover the plugs, it will operate in a pouring rain because the distributor is sealed--but it will not run underwater because the generator and engine breathers are not sealed and the engine would short out and/or fill the crankcase with water. There is no simple, inexpensive method of doing this--but then, how great is the need?

There is some confusion as to what should be done with the generator on a VW engine to be run off the road. First, consider that the engine cooling fan is driven by the generator shaft. The front of the generator is open to permit entry of cooling air. At the rear of the generator there are two long slots in the case over the commutator area. These allow air to exit the generator. One of the things NOT to do is place a strap over these two slots because this traps dust and dirt in the back of the generator, letting it grind into the brushes and commutator.

Make a small piece of metal to fit under the hold-down strap and back past the upper slot, but spaced away from the case by at least 1/4 inch. Thus rocks, dirt, twigs, etc., cannot fall into the slot and small particles can be blown out through the space between case and sheet-metal guard. Leave the lower slot alone so small debris may fall out of the generator. An alternative to this is to glue a section of the polyurethane over the top slot with Silastic RTV.

Now all we've got to do is to keep trash from entering the front of the generator. This we can do only to a degree. On the lip of sheet metal which extends forward at the cooling fan, braze or strap a section of hardware cloth or other metal mesh. This prevents sticks, rocks and other objects from being sucked into the cooling fan and blown either into the generator or between the cylinders to cut off cooling. Several attempts have been made to place a filter in front of the fan shroud and thus eliminate all dust and dirt from the cooling system. The problem here is that to be effective, the filter must be restrictive and thus the already overworked cooling system starves for air and the engine runs hot. This you can do without.

Under the choking layer of Mexican dust you'll find another attempt at reaching for some clean air. Flex hose clamped to stock air cleaner body is routed inside the car to still another air cleaner. There is a throttle return spring for each carb and one for the main linkage, just in case.

Dry element tractor-type air filters come in various sizes and shapes and were originally designed for off-road heavy equipment. These filters swirl much of the dirt out of the air. Accumulated dirt drops through a one-way rubber valve when intake-manifold vacuum drops. A remote mounted filter is a good way to get cleaner air, but long hoses sharply reduce air flow and can hurt engine performance. Extensive bracing to carburetor base and to fan housing is good idea. This Donaldson filter is shown in a cut away on page 39.

From time to time, unbolt the fan shroud--
especially if you have been in brush and weeds--
and thoroughly clean out debris jammed into the
oil cooler and on the cylinder fins. A duct could
be extended from the front of the engine to extend
upward into a cleaner air stream, away from
rocks and grit thrown back by the front wheels.
Window screen on the duct opening will keep out
rocks, snakes, and low-flying birds.

Engine oil should be changed with great frequency
in any off-road engine and the VW stands at the
very top of this list because the engines are not
equipped with oil filters. Thoroughly clean the
screen located just below the oil pickup tube in
the crankcase, flush the case out with solvent
and refill with a quality detergent oil. There are
several accessory oil filter kits on the market
for the VW engine. These are wise investments
if the filters are changed at close and regular
intervals. If this is not your intent, why bother
to throw your money down two drains, buying the
filter kit and frequently rebuilding the engine because of neglect. Toilet-paper filters cannot be
recommended because their "filter" element was
designed for an entirely different purpose.

A full-flow oil filter for the VW engine provides
greatly improved engine life. This installation
is detailed in "How to Hotrod VW Engines. "

Always keep in mind that excessive heat means
death to an engine and the problem of effectively
cooling an air-cooled engine in a high load situation is always difficult. Your off-road VW engine
needs all the help you can give it with a clean oil
cooler, the correct spark advance (not too much),
black sheet metal (for more effective heat radia-
tion), and a cooling flow of air. The latter two
factors are almost never thought of by the off-
road crowd. A simple fact of life is that a
pretty chrome engine runs warmer than a black

one. In a water-cooled engine this may be of
little consequence, but not on a VW engine. The
cooling flow of air is often non-existent on many
dune buggies because sheet metal may have been
removed, and because of careless routing of new
exhaust systems.

The purpose of the sheet metal is to duct the air
so that all the high-temperature areas: heads,
cylinders and oil cooler--can be cooled by a
steady air blast. When the sheet metal is taken
off, the air is not "put to work. " This problem
is compounded by the physical fact that heat
rises. Air for engine cooling and for the carburetor is pulled from the uppermost part of the
engine compartment. On many accessory exhaust systems designed for dune buggies the rear
two exhaust pipes are above the cylinder heads,
closer to both air intakes and closer to the intake
manifold which should be kept cool for the best
horsepower. The cooling system in a sedan is

On stock VWs, crankshaft pulley is threaded on the inner lip. These
threads "screw" the oil back into the crankcase while the engine
is turning to act as an oil seal for the crank. This works so
well that those threads keep right on working when the engine
is running in dirt, water, silt or whathaveyou, screwing it into the
crankcase. Machine the spiral-screw portion of the fan hub to
1.875-inch. Procure a seal adapter from Crower Cams in Chula
Vista, California. Apply a light coat of gasket sealant to the seal
adapter which is a press fit in the end of the case. Then press in
the seal and re-install the crankshaft pulley on the end of the
crank. Engine need not be removed from the car for this operation.
No machining is required on the engine case.

far more sensible. A sheetmetal "waistline"
prevents the air heated by the exhaust from ris-
ing into the engine compartment.

Even the rubber seals around the spark plug
holes are very important. They should be replaced if worn or cracked.

Spark plug seals (boots) are essential for VW, Porsche and Corvair engine cooling. Make sure that these are new and correctly
installed, or your engine will get less cooling than it requires.

Chroming won't make it go faster, but this housing from a McCulloch supercharger installation fully encloses the carburetor to keep all dirt out. We expect these to become exceedingly rare because they are so great for the off-road engine compartment.

Standard Chevrolet racing part — an old air cleaner can be used inside the sedan for an air intake and cleaner. This can't be beat for cleaning efficiency when late paper element is combined with a poly-foam "sock." Notice the roll bar attachment, padding and shoulder harness.

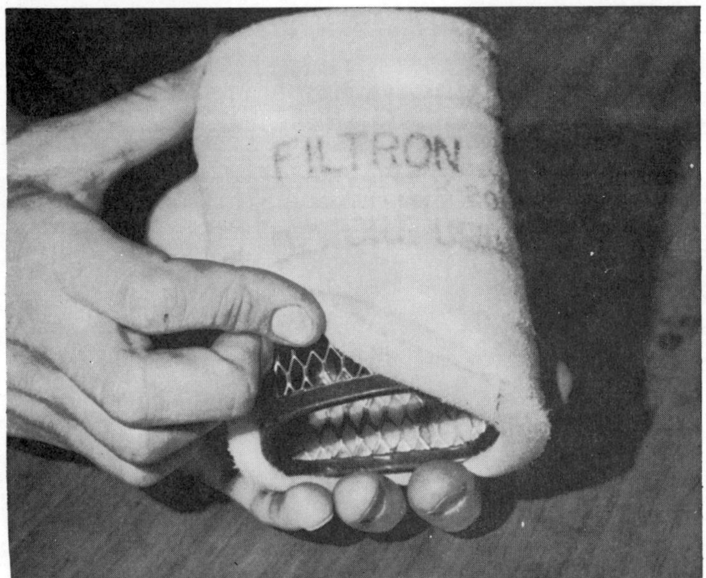

One of several polyurethane filter elements which are seeing increased use off the road. The foam element is supported by the wire screen and is sealed at the top and bottom by the filter can. These filters must never be run dry, but should be coated with an oil especially designed to trap dirt. One of the features of the wet-foam filter element is the fact that it may be cleaned in solvent, re-oiled and used many times.

Some off-roaders are starting the movement to house the entire carburetor in a dust-proof container. When this is done, the carburetor sits inside a clean-air area so that its shaft ends and choke -- as well as air bleeds -- never get dusty. All of the air which comes into the housing is first cleaned up by the air filter. Thus, the housing must have an entry for a hose to the air cleaner and sealed entries for the fuel line, and the choke and throttle cables. Sealed openings for wrench access are also necessary, of course. The first of these units which have been observed on off-road vehicles have been made from the housings which were supplied with McCulloch Superchargers. However, it is relatively easy to make a housing out of aluminum.

The simple approach is that of making the base-plate match the manifold stud pattern. Then the carburetor can be used as the clamping device to secure the housing. Longer carburetor mounting studs may be needed, and aircraft-style self-locking nuts are suggested because the fasteners are out of sight and hence apt to be neglected.

Still another approach places the carburetor inside of a deep air cleaner, with the fuel line, throttle cable and choke cable entering the enclosure through the baseplate. With this set up, the carburetor is accessible by merely taking off the top plate, which holds the assembly together.

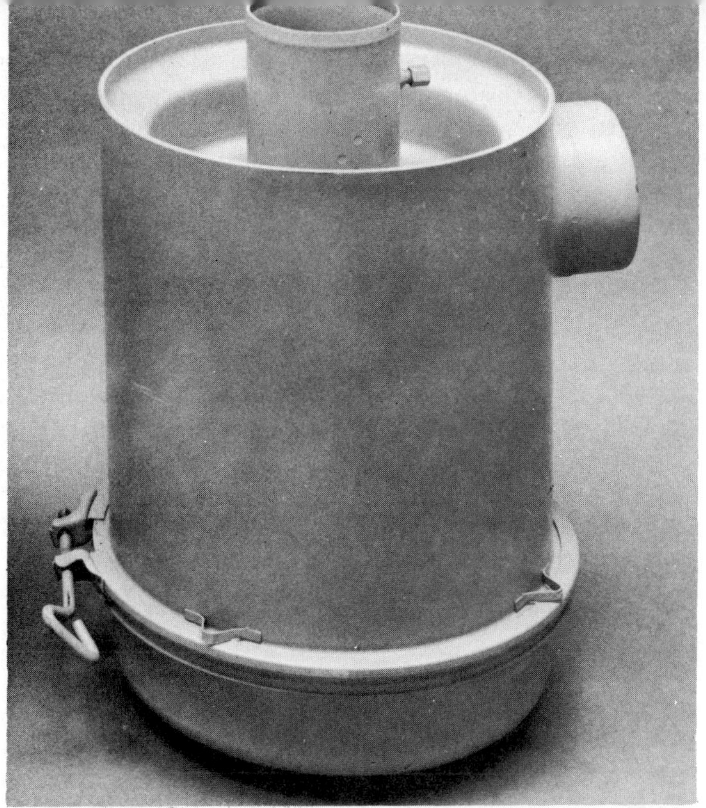

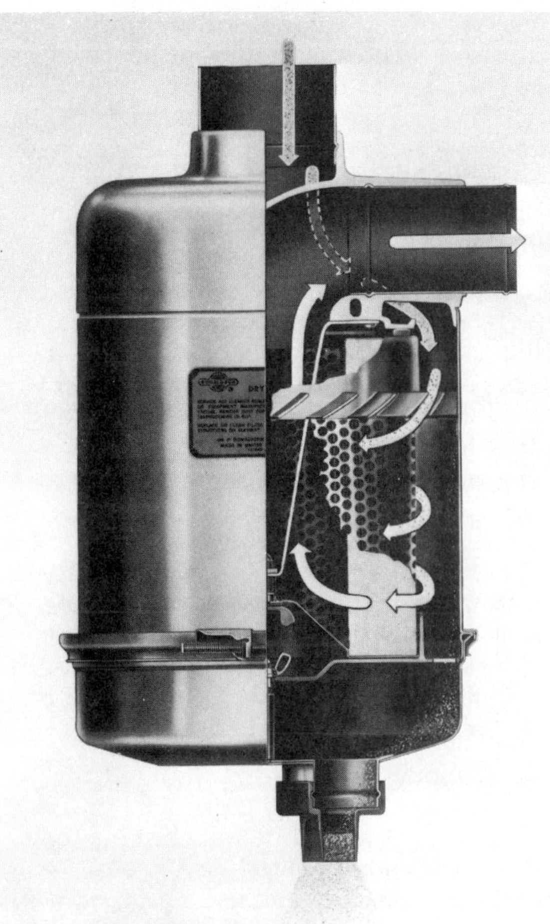

CYCLOPAC Air Cleaners are made in horizontal and vertical models by Donaldson Co. of Minneapolis. Truck and heavy-equipment dealers have these available in several sizes to fit dune-buggy engines. These combine centrifugal action with a paper element to achieve 99% cleaning efficiency. Price is about $28 for the 5¼″ diameter model which weighs five pounds. Arrows show air flow.

Most of the dirt which gets into an off-road engine is pulled in by the intake system, placing a heavy burden on the air cleaner. Since off-roading started getting much-deserved notice in the motoring publications, manufacturers have been falling over themselves to tell the enthusiasts about "the" air cleaner to use off the road.

Most off-roaders, especially racers, expect too much of any filter. They strap one on, perhaps even a good one, then run the vehicle without properly installing the filter in the first place or without servicing the air-cleaning system. For most off-road VW engine applications, the stock oil-bath filter is entirely adequate for the job-- IF the filter can is sealed tightly against the carburetor throat and IF the oil is changed quite frequently. For operation in dusty (desert) terrain, several improvements can be made to the air-cleaning system.

Despite the type of accessory filter chosen, the filter should be located to take in "cleaner" air. This means the filter should go higher (away from the wheels) and forward (still further from the large, churning rear wheels). On a sedan the filter can be attached to the top of the roof or inside the car. Inside mounting is noisier, but protects the filter if there's a rollover. Noise is a disconcerting by-product of placing the filter inside a bodied car, so think of that before putting the filter inside your sedan. On a glass-bodied car, the filter element is almost always located on the roll bar or roll cage. The cleaner should be mounted below the contact point so that the filter won't be destroyed in a rollover. The car can usually be righted and driven away, but a damaged air filter will allow sanding the engine and that will cause it to stop.

Despite the type and final location, if a remote mounting is chosen, a connection must be made between the air cleaner and the carb throat. Look at some of the ideas presented photographically within these pages. Consider some bitter facts before making a decision. The longer the connecting hose, pipe or whatever, the more friction or resistance to air travel will be present, and this steals horsepower. The more fittings used, the more fittings and joints which must be sealed air tight with clamps, tape, glue or putty. Long pieces of pipe, hose, or tubing must be clamped or tied into place with great care. One good split between filter and carburetor and your filter becomes worthless. The hose can collapse due to the low pressure created by the engine intake, and reduce or even choke the engine completely. Taping the hose will usually prevent it from collapsing.

The effectiveness of the various filter types: paper or foam--or centrifugal with either element type is not soon to be resolved by off-roaders. Alliances have been formed and loyalties cemented in this area and opinions are hard to change. Factual information is almost impossible to gather--because of differences in servicing a cleaning system.

Try these tips and you'll be close. Apply a layer of thick wheel-bearing grease to the upper and lower sealing-edge surfaces of either paper or the polyurethane foam elements: Check often to see that the sealing surfaces on the element and on the element holder are not warped or distorted. If the filter element can be cleaned, follow the manufacturer's directions to the letter. Check all hoses, clamps and mounting brackets often for cracks, leaks or possible mount failure. Get a filter element large enough to do the job. The drugstore-cowboy, chrome-topped wonder that was a press fit on a '49 Ford two barrel will not get the job done. Such items are of little help on the street, much less off the road.

A remote, accessory-type filter is a must for off-road VW engines with a carb perched on each head. In a glass car, any air cleaner mounted directly above the head-mounted carburetor is almost directly in line with everything thrown off the rear wheels--a chronic problem for those running Porsche or Corvair engines off the road. This is asking far too much of any filter.

So plan to use a remote air/filter on your off-road engine if dual carbs are to be run on an open-wheeled glass-bodied car.

Simple Filtron "wet sock" cleaner on mid-engined buggy cuts complexity to a minimum. Such simplicity helps to offset the few extra percent efficiency provided by a polyfoam-plus-paper unit.

The AC Spark Plug Division of General Motors has supplied the following information which helps to separate fact from the fictions to which we have all been exposed. In summary, it would appear that the current trend towards the combining of a polyurethane "sock" around a paper-element filter may be as "near-perfect" a combination as can be had.

AC points out that proper filtration of air prior to its entrance into the engine reduces fouling of carburetor parts and spark plugs, and reduces wear on engine parts: pistons, piston rings, cylinder walls, and bearings.

Even a VW engine can consume an entire "box car" full of air in just 24 minutes. If driving conditions were considered hazardous because of dust clouds reducing visibility, then our box car full of air would contain at least a handful of dust.

Air cleaners are classified into general groups based on the principle of filtration and the "condition" of the filtering material. AC makes oil-wetted metal, oil bath, dry paper, wetted paper, polyurethane foam and "dual-state" or paper-polyfoam combinations.

Oil-Wetted Metal - Filtering material is a relatively coarse entanglement of crinkled aluminum ribbon, coated with a film of oil--usually by dipping in clean engine oil and allowing to drain. As a particle of dust tries to penetrate the element, it strikes an oiled surface of the ribbon and sticks. This process continues until all of the oil has been soaked up and the dirt particles no longer stick when they strike the dry, dust-covered ribbons.

Publisher's Note: This type of filter has a low first cost and is not very efficient. It should not be even considered for an off-road vehicle.

Oil Bath - Here again, dust particles are collected on an oily surface. In this case, the filter element is a pad of densely entwined cactus fibers positioned directly over a pool of oil. The incoming dirty air is forced to reverse its direction over this oil before entering the element. In making a 180° turn over the pool of oil, many dust particles strike the oil and stay there. Oil mist which is carried into the element by the air stream washes off and re-oils the filtering fibers.

Oil-bath cleaners are expensive. They are big and bulky. Some form of splash protection is required to keep the oil from leaving the reservoir when the vehicle stops suddenly, starts suddenly or bounces on uneven terrain. A sustained vehicle attitude such as on a long hill or in a pit will alter the oil level within the air cleaner, impairing its function.

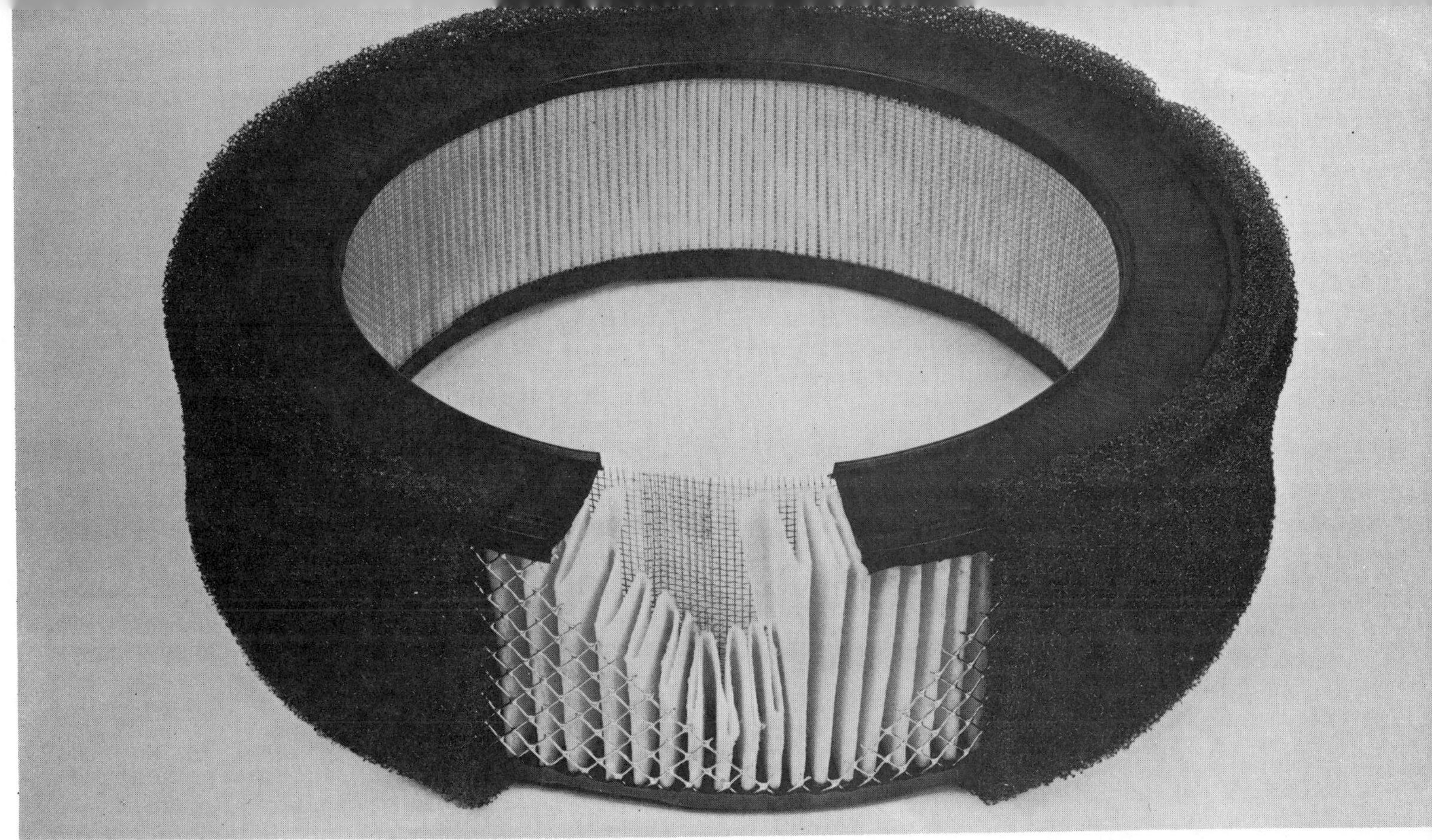

AC 222 C dual-stage filter is used on some Chevy Blazers and big trucks. It measures 5¾ x 12¼ inches and costs about $10 as Chevy P/N 6421326. This filter is too big for most housings, so AC 223 C which is only 2⅞ inches high (with same 12¼ inch diameter) is better — and cheaper as Chevy P/N 6422680 at $8.25.

The filter element must be oil wetted to perform its function, consequently the oil bath air cleaner must be designed to draw oil mist into the element at reasonably low air flows at or near engine idle conditions. On the other hand, at high engine speeds the air flow must not be permitted to draw the oil completely through the element and carry the dirt into the engine.

Unless the oil level is maintained accurately, the oil mist will not be drawn into the filter element at the designed air flow rate, leaving the engine unprotected. If long periods elapse between servicings, dirt displaces oil in the reservoir, raises the level and lowers the pull-over point (the air flow rate at which oil is drawn through the element into the engine). The result is a sudden and infinitely more harmful dose of dirt thrown into the engine, and the filter becomes almost completely useless immediately thereafter. Average efficiency of an oil-bath cleaner at 150 CFM is 95%, increasing with flow.

Dry - Until the early '60's, dry paper was considered the best air filter on the market for passenger car and light-truck usage. The protection given to the engine in terms of keeping dirt out of the intake system was superior to any other readily available filter on the market.

An impregnated paper composed mainly of cotton and rayon fibers is not in any way oiled and relies on its dense structure to act as a strainer. Its "pore size" is very small and only a few of the "holes" are even as large as a human hair. Although this type of element "plugs up" faster than the other two, this "clogging" action is retarded because many of the dust particles adhere to the filtering fibers.

Overall laboratory efficiency of dry-type cleaners is about 98% and does not vary appreciably with variations in air flow. Initial restriction is about the same as wetted aluminum mesh and somewhat less than an oil-bath unit. Although dust capacities vary considerably with size, an oil-bath unit has many times the capacity of a dry-type unit. However, the dry type will protect the engine religiously even until the engine will no longer run due to lack of air.

If cleaned with expert care, dry-type elements may be re-used several times. AC recommends that these filter elements be replaced by new ones when engine performance is impaired as indicated by an AC paper-element air-cleaner tester.

Wetted Polyurethane - These filters came next, starting around 1960. The wettant gave polyurethane the increase in efficiency over dry polyurethane necessary for automotive usage. This element offered even more engine protection than dry paper. To assure consistent high performance of this element, a special wettant was developed for application at the factory. This wettant had greater adhesion to polyurethane than the oils which had previously been used. This assured that the wettant would be retained on the element and provide high dust-collecting performance.

Even though these polyurethane elements gave superior engine protection, the dust capacity was less than that of dry-paper elements on some road tests... there was still room for improvement.

Wetted Paper - For 1964 cars, AC engineered and released improved paper elements with increased efficiency and dirt capacity. The improvement resulted from wetting the paper with oil as part of the manufacturing process.

Numerous tests showed that the dust capacity was doubled and that the oil treatment also increased the efficiency of the paper over a wide range of dust-particle sizes.

The final tests were based on field results in which oiled-paper elements were run in direct comparisons against dry elements at the G. M. Desert Proving Ground in Arizona under extremely severe conditions. The oiled-paper elements consistently out-performed the dry-paper and wetted-polyurethane elements. The dirt capacity of oiled paper is double that of dry paper and more than double that of wetted polyurethane. Examination of interior air-cleaner and carburetor surfaces shows them to be much cleaner when an oiled-paper element has been used.

Dual-Stage - This air-cleaner type was developed as an improvement over the oil bath type used on trucks in heavy-duty operations with severe dust conditions.

The Dual-Stage air cleaner provides improved protection against engine wear due to dust. This is due to the high filtration efficiency of the wetted paper secondary stage. Dual-Stage elements have a filter efficiency of 99. 5% compared to AC and other oil-bath cleaners which range from 86. 6% to 98. 6% efficient.

These air cleaners require less frequent servicing because they hold more dust. The following chart compares Dual-Stage air cleaners (used by Chevrolet) with other conventional elements and oil-bath air cleaners for the same engines.

Air Cleaner	Dust Capacity @ 5" Restriction Increase @ 200 cfm	Filtering Efficiency
Dual-Stage	772 grams	99. 5%
Dry Paper	120 grams	98. 2%
Oil-Wetted Paper	263 grams	99. 4%
Oil Bath	300 grams	98. 6%

This data indicates that Dual-Stage elements have over six times the capacity of dry paper, three times that of oil-wetted paper, and two times the capacity of an oil-bath type.

The paper and outer wrap filter design is a two-stage filter containing Glycol-wetted polyurethane (at least 1/2" thick) backed with oiled pleated filter paper. This integral construction of filter paper, polyurethane, backfire and support screens all embedded in plastisol and seals is similar in size and shape to dry-type paper filters containing pleated paper only.

This filter's performance characteristics, particularly its dirt-holding capability, make it suited for passenger car installations in areas where severe dust conditions are encountered.

Relative merits of air-cleaner types:

TYPE	EFFICIENCY	SERVICE LIFE	COST
Centrifugal*	Poor	Long	High
Aluminum Mesh	Poor	Long	Low
Oil Bath	Good	Long	High
Polyurethane (wetted)	Good	Medium	Medium
Paper (wetted)	Excellent	Medium	Medium
Paper-Poly	Excellent	Medium to Long	Medium

*Publisher's Note: AC's comparison is "unfair to present-day centrifugal filters which combine centrifugal action with a paper element to get very high efficiency."

Two electric fuel pumps on this racing sedan are a relatively inexpensive form of insurance. Stock VW mechanical pump is also retained with plastic block modifications as described in H. P. Books "How to Hotrod VW Engines."

Non-hardening body putty may be used effectively to seal dirt and water out of the distributor. Exhaust-header nuts have been tack welded to prevent backing off from vibration. Drilling the nuts and using safety wire makes more sense if you want to be able to remove parts without a chisel or cutting torch.

Spare coil is also carried — ready to take over if the number one unit gives up. In such a case, make sure you understand how to effect the hookup in the field without the need of additional wires. Both coils can be equipped with plastic connectors to make the swap a simple pull-push-click operation.

The constant battle is to keep sand and grit from the inside of the engine. Notice the consistent use of electrical and duct tape to provide a dust and moisture tight seal. Duct tape ensures that oil-filler cap won't vibrate off and even seals in dipstick.

Another version of a round-tube nerf bar assembly. Air cleaner has been made from a large metal can and an aluminum pot lid. Give some thought to this if you plan to fabricate your own. Should the cleaner shake apart while you're way down the road, you can run out of duct tape before the problem is solved.

Hydraulic throttle linkage is being used on an increasing number of off-road vehicles. These expensive units represent complexity and cannot be easily fixed when miles from home. They are as trouble prone as cable-actuated units. Rear slots of generator have been taped closed which will trap sand in the generator and reduce generator cooling.

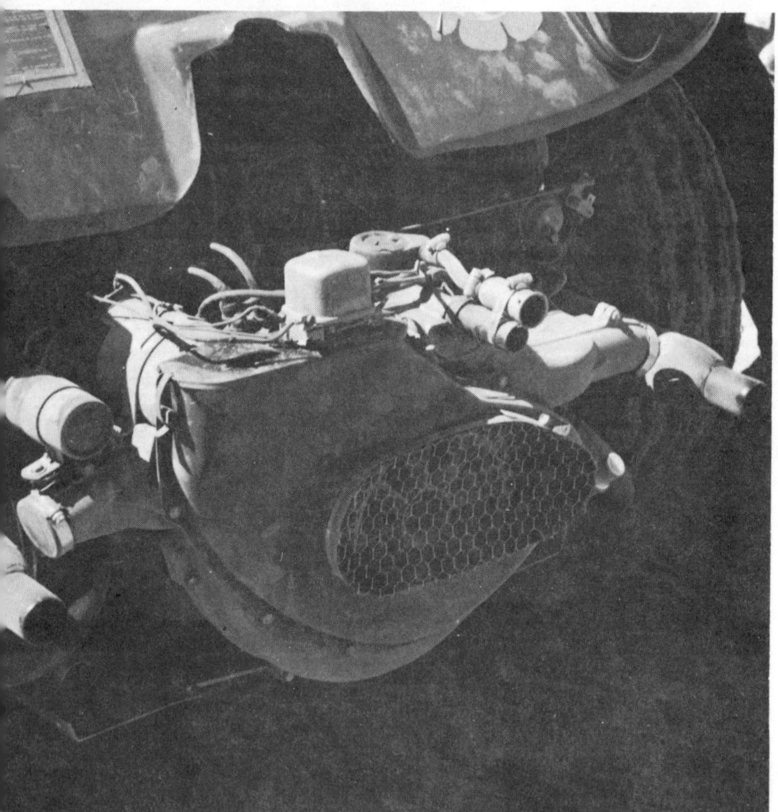

Small-mesh chicken wire strapped across the air inlet on this Variant engine keeps weeds, rocks, sticks and kids' hands out of the blower. This is also recommended for all upright off-road VW engines. Wire is retained with a big worm-screw clamp. Clamped covers on unused heater-air outlets ensure that all of the cooling air is available for cooling the engine. Don't let screen clog up!

TRI-PHASE is another centrifugal plus paper element filter which is popular for sand duners and off-roaders.

Top: Disassembled TRI-PHASE Filter has internal paper element which can be replaced when loaded with dirt. Rubber valve at end of "spin" housing expels excess dirt accumulation. Left: Hardware cloth or other close-mesh wire screen clamped in place over cooling-air inlet prevents debris from getting through the fan and onto the head and cylinder fins. Fan housing has extra brace as insurance against off-road bouncing. Above: Duct tape seals carb to air-cleaner fitting and also seals fitting to flex hose which extends inside of sedan (or buggy) body to a remote filter.

Comparison of Corvair air filters. Four-carb engines (140HP) are best fitted with the stock arrangement (top left) which mounts filter over engine center, has less parts, and is therefore less failure prone. Crown kits should be used to seal throttle shafts. Above: Polyfoam filter elements are tough to adapt so that everything fits perfectly to keep out dirt. Segmented belt used here is wrong for Corvairs. Left: Center-mounted carb is out of the way of sand and dirt flung off of the rear wheels, but suffers "bog" unless modified as described in our Corvair book.

Renault engines also power a lot of "scratch-built" off-the-road equipment.

Single seaters are the off-road racers of the future. This one's even more futuristic with its mid-engine location.

Extra fuel capacity can be added within confines of VW trunk. Tank can fill without raising hood. All of that wiring is extremely vulnerable. Protect it or keep out those things which could cut or fray wiring.

Talk about complexity. This set up does not get more low-end torque from Webers or any other carburetor set up. The owner never heard of Kettering's famous slogan, *"Parts left out cost nothing and cause no service problems."*

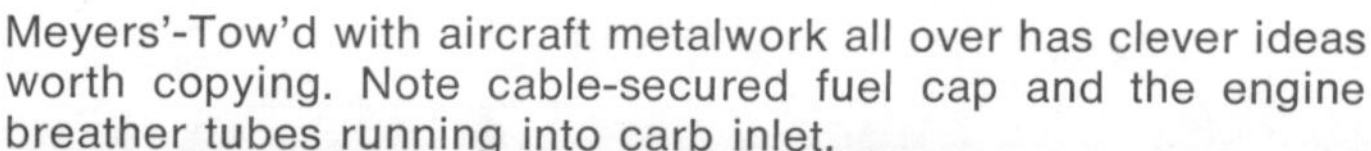

Meyers'-Tow'd with aircraft metalwork all over has clever ideas worth copying. Note cable-secured fuel cap and the engine breather tubes running into carb inlet.

Channel-iron runners under this Corvair may be great psychological protection, but offer no actual safety for the underside of the engine. The exhaust, oil pan, and push rod tubes are all vulnerable with this set up, so don't take it off the street. More on skid plates on page 68.

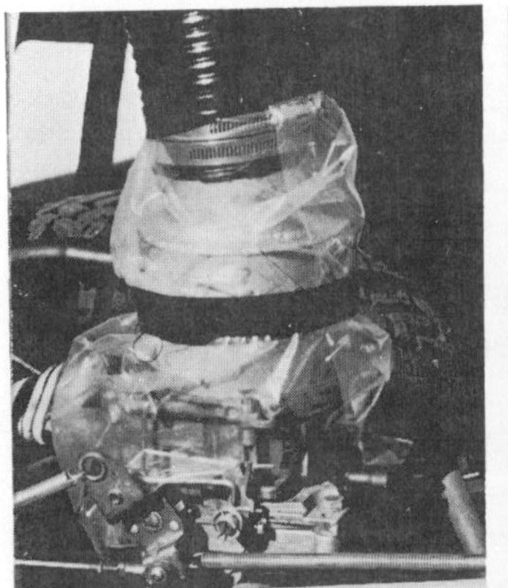

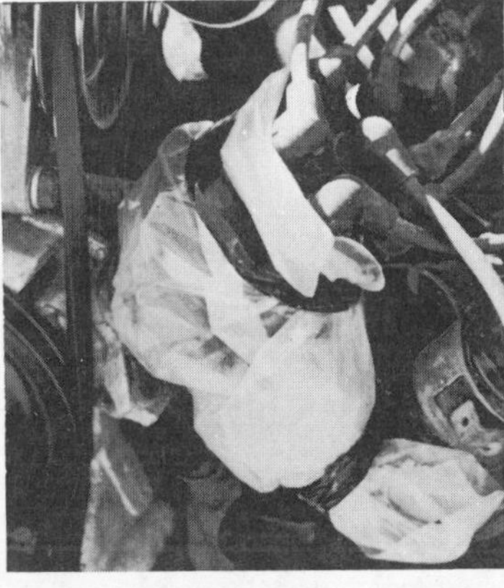

Baggy plastic covers keep dust out of this carburetor and distributor. This is not a recommended "fix" because the plastic is easily torn.

Air-cleaner securely mounted to sedan's backside keeps noise out of cab, but is vulnerable.

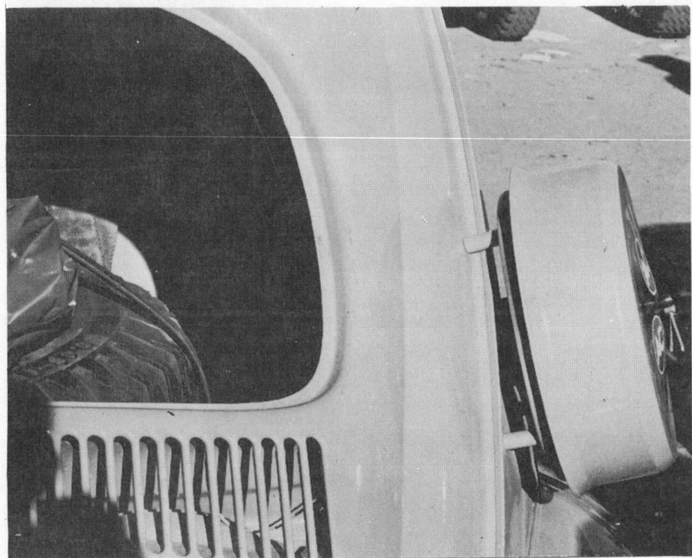

Skid plate under Ford V-4 industrial engine curves up at back to protect sump, pulley and accessory-drive casting.

If you are running this tiny cooler on your Corvair-powered buggy or sedan — better read our book "How to Hotrod Corvair Engines." It details all four Corvair coolers, all eight engines (80HP through 180HP) and covers a lot of details for off-road preparation.

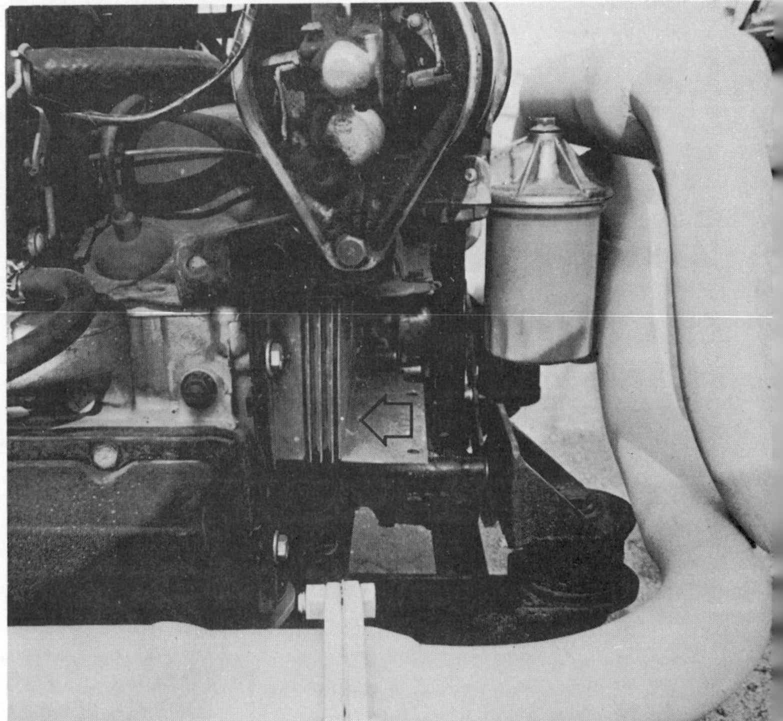

Many special driving lights come with plastic covers which are held on with rubber straps. Use tape to make doubly sure that the covers don't fall off.

Map light on flexible "stalk" is a super-handy item when you are trying to read that map. Be sure to fold your maps so that the area of interest is visible through celluloid sheet protectors which are available in stationery stores. That keeps the wind from blowing the map around.

Mounting lights on a chopped-off sedan can challenge the imagination. Here are solutions to the problem.

Four CIBIE quartz-iodine lights are mounted low on this single-seat Baja racer. Steel U-channel mount is welded to shock towers.

Off-Road
Electrics,
Instruments
& Lights

We'd wager that those who drive motor vehicles off-road spend more time solving electrical problems than any other. Again, with time and common sense, the VW electrical system can virtually be "bullet proofed."

Wires fall off. Of course they will if the connector is a push fit onto a terminal. Use full eyelet-type connectors with the wire firmly crimped into place with the correct crimping tool. Use the correct size wire to fit the connector. Solder all connections for a competition car. Use a drop of Loctite on the nut when attaching the connector to the terminal block.

Wires short out. Sure, you can throw a lug wrench, a jack and a piece of chain on top of two camp stools inside the trunk of a VW sedan going off the road. But when you drive it around off the road for a week, the chances of some of that stuff breaking or rubbing a wire in two are good. Wherever a wire passes through a hole in a panel, put it through a section of rubber tubing or use a rubber grommet. Plenty of electrical tape can also be used. Don't let wire move around behind the instrument panel, in the engine compartment, or anywhere in between. A dozen or so Adel clips from the local hardware or surplus outlet will go a long way in keeping wire tied down and out of the way. An electronics supply firm will stock several items which can be used to hold wire in place.

On buggies and sedans, tighten down the instrument-mounting bolts and give the threads the liquid-rubber treatment. Instruments have been known to fall out of the dashboard carrying wire and a shower of sparks toward the driver's feet. This always happens at night, quite possibly in the rain and almost always going up a steep grade. Need we say more?

Those really serious about doing the job correctly will replace all switches with marine items constructed to seal out moisture and corrosion. Most of the off-road racing crowd goes this route and then runs a bead of trim cement or liquid rubber around the joint between the non-conductive switch back and the metal switch box.

Old-style knife switches actually are better because you can always short across the terminals and they are self-cleaning.

Stock VW instruments are adequate for normal off-road use. Make certain that the generator warning light is working properly. This warns if the generator is still "genning," which is of secondary importance to whether the cooling fan is turning. If the belt breaks or comes off, the red light should go on. When this occurs the cooling fan is out of business and the engine will quickly overheat and seize. One clever idea is to wire the horn into the generator-warning light so that the horn blows as soon as the red light comes on, giving you a double warning to stop and check for trouble.

Or, you might take a tip from some of the English sedan racers (minis, would you believe?) who wire clearance lights on their dashboards to serve as warnings for loss of oil pressure, alternator trouble and so forth. With this kind of searchlight in front of you, even in the daytime, you would have to be "on pills" to miss the signal.

Oil pressure, oil temperature and vacuum indicators and a tachometer are all worthwhile instruments, but are not mandatory for an off-road vehicle. When working with a race car, on or off-road, a lot can be learned quickly by watching these instruments under various terrain and engine loading situations. The writers of this book lean toward the philosophy embodied in "Boss" Kettering's statement (he was a famous GM engineer)--"Parts left out cost nothing and cause no service problems." Think about that one constantly when preparing any off-road or racing vehicle.

The instruments which you can buy for your buggy or sedan are typically more susceptible to vibration and failure than the systems which they are supposed to protect.

Pre-1967 VW electrical systems were six-volt. These systems consistently cause trouble off-road when considerable night driving is done. This system was not designed for use with the high-intensity, high-candlepower driving lights which are often added to an off-road machine. The six-volt system can be converted to 12 volt by changing the generator field coils, the voltage regulator and the coil to 12-volt VW items. Or, a complete 12-volt generator can be installed if the coil and voltage regulator are also changed. Most of the enthusiasts who do this leave the starter alone and run a full 12-volt system--all instruments, lights, etc. --but leaving the six-volt starter. This is a sound plan because the starter will now spin much faster--a real help in a hard-start situation. Don't be tempted to use low-cost voltage dropping resistors to power your wipers, instruments and radio (on an off-road vehicle--that's ridiculous!) Voltage-dropping resistors sound simple and they are. Unfortunately, the voltage which they provide varies with the load of the device which is being powered. A 4. 5-ohm 10 to 25 watt resistor is needed in series for the wiper; and a 7. 5-ohm 10 to 25 watt resistor for a transistor-type radio. Using a six-volt radio on 12 volts requires careful setting of a variable resistor in about a 100-watt size to get precisely six volts into the radio.

Dropping diodes are a better way to be sure that you are getting precisely six volts. If you have a friend who is an electronics engineer or technician, he can help you select and mount the appropriate diodes. No wires need to be changed when making the 6-to-12 switchover.

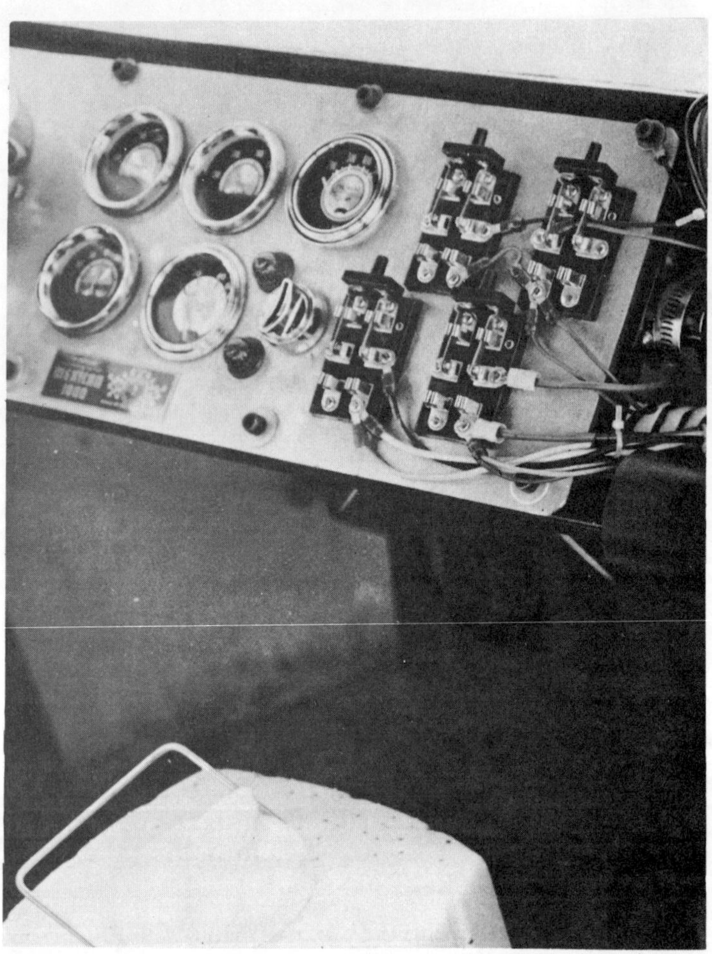

Knife switches are inexpensive, positive and reliable. A fiberglas cover hinged over these would save the passenger's face in a crash. Use of closed-cell insulation on steering brake and shift levers is described in roll-bar chapter. If you must carry a passenger, a grab bar becomes essential. Use of instruments for a buggy is questionable. Idiot lights are more reliable and less likely to give false indications.

High-candlepower driving lights are helpful off-the-road additions. Many types, sizes and shapes are available at all prices, and oddly enough, the price seems to be in inverse proportion to the amount of light actually produced by the lamp. Do some shopping and some testing-- and some reading. Driving lights have been discussed in the following articles:

AUXILIARY LIGHTS, ROAD & TRACK, Mar. 69.

LIGHTING THE WAY, by Chris Peek
ROAD & TRACK, May 1969

MORE ABOUT AUXILIARY LIGHTS
ROAD & TRACK, June 1968

Some new illumination on an opaque subject, by Martin A.Jackson (discusses fog lights)
CAR LIFE, December 1966

See and be seen, by Martin A. Jackson, a four-part article in CAR LIFE, Sept., Oct., Nov. and Dec. 1963

THE BETTER TO SEE YOU WITH, by Wally Wyss, CAR LIFE, February 1970

TAKE YOUR PICK: Fog Lamps
The MOTOR, November 27, 1963

Lights should be mounted high to keep from getting broken and to add dimension to the terrain so you can better judge how deep a hole is. The driving lights are of two basic types: a pencil-beam lens and a wide flat diffuser lens. One of each type used with the stock VW lights makes an adequate setup for most off-road driving. Make certain you are not exceeding the capabilities of the generating system when you begin adding lights. You must know how much power each light needs. Always wire auxiliary lights on a separate switch for each light so that each type of light can be used only when needed.

On the other hand, fog presents different set of problems, requiring that the go-fast-in-fog lights be mounted low. The PER-LUX lights which are often seen on big trucks have proved to be an excellent choice for the fogs encountered in Baja, Southern California and Nevada. These include a high-candlepower sealed beam unit combined with a set of baffles to keep the light rays from any upward spreading. As with the other lights on a buggy or sedan, these should be kept covered with foam rubber and masking tape (or duct tape) during the day when they are not needed. Rocks do manage to find the lighting equipment with alarming regularity.

A hand-controlled spotlight mounted high on the vehicle is sometimes more useful than any number of driving lights because of its controllability and flexibility. Some units can still be found in wrecking yards on older cars. A plug-in, hand-held trouble light is also a valuable addition to any off-road vehicle. These can be purchased in most any auto store for a few dollars. Get one with enough cord to stretch to any point on the vehicle for tire changing or troubleshooting the engine.

Experienced off-road racers put a shield under each light which is mounted high, thereby making sure that the light will not bounce off of the car to create glare for the occupants. They also paint the surfaces forward of the driver and passenger, making everything in sight flat black.

Another light which should be included is a map light for the navigator -- or for the driver in a single-seat car. The navigator should be able to use this light without distracting the driver.

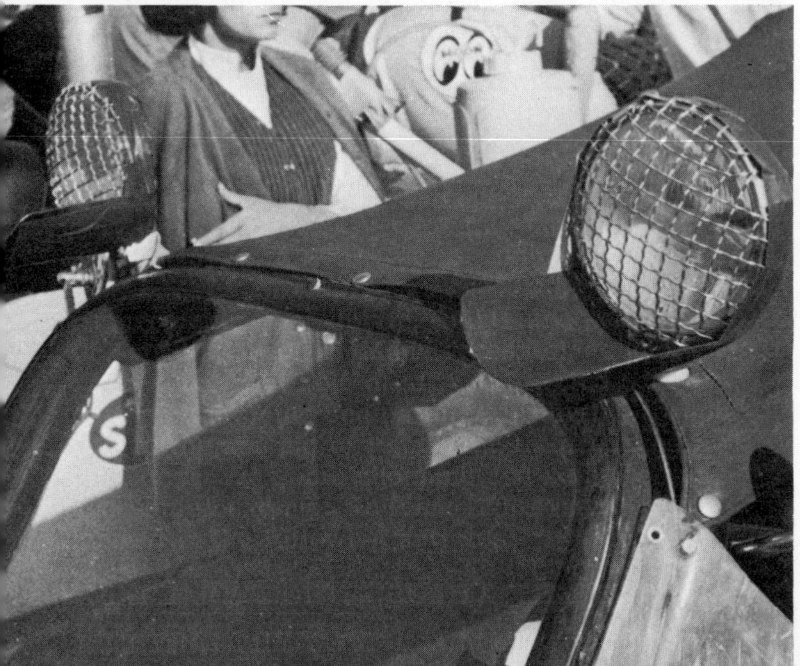

Shields screwed and duct-taped in place to keep glare away from occupants.

PER-LUX fog lights are mounted low for best fog penetration. Pencil-beam lights are only used when there's no fog.

1969 Baja 1000 cars. Above: alternator installed as a spare. Right: alternator belted to extra crankshaft pulley for primary source of charging current.

Another possibility which has worked out quite well for some of the more progressive-thinking off-road racers is the use of two small size (but high amperage) aircraft batteries in conjunction with a sealed marine switch which allows the use of either or both batteries. Thus one battery may be run down and the system switched to the fresh battery, or both can be switched on to overcome a difficult starting situation.

Shop for an extra-service high-ampere-hour battery if you plan to use large driving lights or if the vehicle sits idle much of the time. As a guide, the stock six-volt VW battery is a 77-ampere-hours unit, but larger heavy-duty batteries are available with up to 120 amp hours or so in reasonable sizes and weights. While heavy-service truck and tractor batteries offer still more amp hours, their weight and size preclude using them in a sedan or buggy. Leave those for the drag racers who have to put them in their trunks for extra traction and weight transfer. In any buggy or sedan being driven off road, make certain that you have a strongly constructed battery mount which will contain the battery under all conditions. Only a tiny amount of vertical or horizontal movement will allow the heavy battery to beat itself to death. The side or bottom of the case will crack and allow the acid to escape. While it may be tempting to buy two cheap batteries and connect them in parallel to double the capacity, remember the old adage about parts left out costing nothing and causing no service problems. Extra pieces are re-

quired to mount and connect two batteries. Be sure that your battery is grounded to the trans-axle. Cleaning the ground point and the ground connection is an excellent idea.

Add up the amps or watts drawn by your lights, ignition and other electrical equipment — and you may find that the total is greater than can be supplied by the 6-volt, 200-watt VW generator. You may also discover that some of the accessory driving lights are only available in 12-volt units. Watts, in case you didn't remember, are the product of volts X amperes. Thus the VW generator's 200 watts, divided by 6 volts, translates into 33 amps nominal output at about 1,100 RPM engine speed. What can you do when you need more than 33 amps — or 12 volts for your high-intensity lighting equipment? 12 volts is not a problem if you are starting with a 67 or later VW — not usual for an off-road car, of course. Getting those extra amps is another story.

Some serious off-road competitors are mounting alternators as spares for the VW generator or as the primary source of charging current. We believe that there is still a better idea, but before discussing our "ideal solution," lets look at the features offered by the alternator, as opposed to a generator. Alternators provide practically full output at idling speed. They are inherently self regulating and are thus less critical as regards voltage regulation over a wide speed range. Finally, some alternators are available with solid-state regulators which have no moving parts and are thus less failure prone — especially in the bounce and vibrate off-road environment.

Junked U. S. autos can provide inexpensive 12-V alternators with outputs ranging from 35 to over 50 amperes, depending on the model. Your near-by auto-electrical store can assist you in making

Alternator with one long belt across stock VW generator to drive cooling fan. Note inlet housing to Weber carburetor. Air cleaner is mounted remotely inside of sedan. Photo made during Baja 1000 Technical Inspection for '69 race.

the correct selection. But, don't look for a super-simple bolt-on kit to add an alternator to your VW engine. You'll just have to make the adapter parts yourself. With Corvairs, there is a different story, as all of these engines from 65 through 69 had alternators as standard parts. Be sure to buy the regulator with the alternator. It will probably be a relay type which is similar to that on your VW system. Don't hesitate to use it. It will be as rugged as any of the others which you'll find — short of the solid-state type — and those are not readily available in junkyards! If you are serious, you'll want to set up your system with dual voltage regulators anyway — almost all competitors do.

Now, about that "ideal solution" we talked about earlier. You can keep your standard 6-volt VW generator and all other standard 6V equipment and still run 12-volt lighting units — without installing a 12V battery. How? By adding the 12V alternator and regulator and using this arrangement to power the lights directly. Because the alternator is not "self-starting," it will get its initial excitation from the accessory wiring of the 6V system through a 10-ohm resistor. Once the alternator is working, lights and other equipment are powered from the alternator — until you stop the engine — when you won't need your driving lights anyway. Right? Here again, simplicity pays off by permitting you to leave out heavy and breakable equipment — such as 12V batteries.

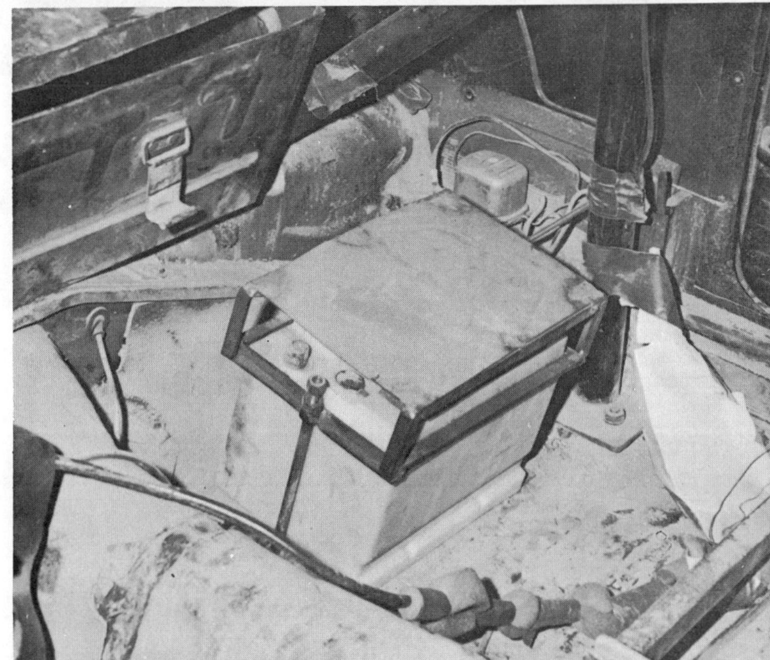

Battery tied to back floorboard of sedan. Angle iron and sheet metal tie down and cover keep battery secure. Innertube seal prevents acid from running onto occupants, even in event of upset. Both batteries have poly-plastic cases which should be less subject to breaking from vibration.

The drivers of this dune buggy off-road racer had some problems along the way but managed to pick up the checkered flag anyway. Notice the driving light mounted on the rear of the roll-cage pointing toward the rear. A light placed here is invaluable when backing up after dark. Roll-cage protects occupants, skid plate at front protects suspension components.

With some machine work and a ballast resistor, the 24-volt coil/distributor unit from a military Mighty Mite installs in a VW engine to provide a completely sealed ignition system. Earth-moving or tractor sales firms stock shielded plugs in a wide variety of sizes and heat ranges. Resistor needed for this conversion is Prestolite 938987. Military surplus yards have the used distributors.

One of the most enthusiastic and talented off-road racers is movie actor James Garner who has teamed up for driving chores with Racer Scooter Patrick on several occasions. Notice the extreme fender cutouts on this buggy. Taped headlights are protected against breakage during the day. Two outboard gas tanks provide a car of this size with a great cruising range. The tall black stack to the rear of the vehicle is an engine air inlet. The theory here is to take in air which is not so full of dust and dirt. Of course, an air filter is still used on the carburetor.

Long shields keep glare from the eyes of the driver and passenger of this 1966 Corvair coupe. Shields are pop riveted to light rim. Extra metal stiffener inside of roof is essential to keep lights from tearing away due to vibration.

Need some light? Have some light! Cowl lamp is 200,000 candle-power-worth of broad flat beam — which really needs a shield to protect driver from glare. Two upper lamps are PER-LUX fog units which would work better if mounted low on bumper. Movable spot on roof is a handy item. This current requirement would cause you to consider using an alternator instead of the stock generator.

Keep it simple. Even if all lights are wired individually, there's no need for a gaggle of switches and knobs on an off-road machine. Electrical shorts or spilled gasoline can cause fires and a junior-size fire extinguisher lashed under the dash could make up for the lack of a local fire department out in the boondocks.

Here are a couple of ideas worth tucking away for a light-duty off-road or sand machine. Corvair passenger-car dual-light unit is easily mounted anywhere on your car. Wire coiled around the bottom of the lights connects into tow vehicle for legal highway towing. Two small channel-iron brackets just inside shock towers are for tow-bar attachment.

Two top photos illustrate super-neat wiring held in place with electronic wire-ties. Note how spares and flares are taped or wire-tied into place. This VW engine has a modified fuel-injection manifold. Other photos illustrate various methods of mounting auxiliary lighting equipment.

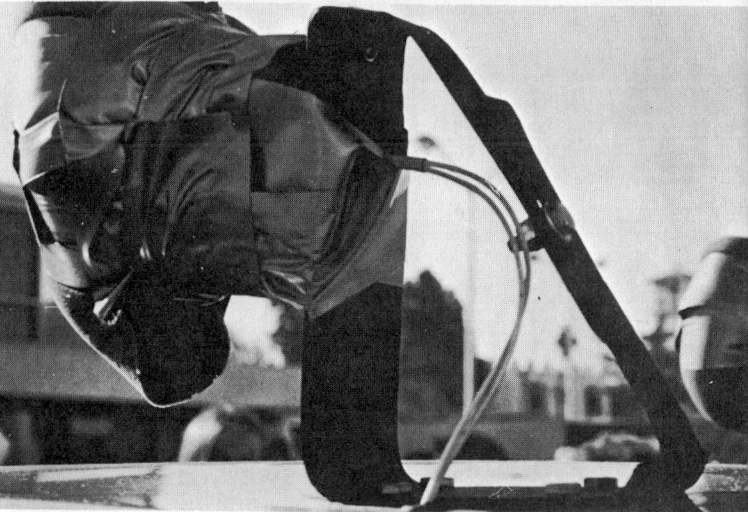

Bumper bar welded to torsion tubes supports front of skid plate and provides tow-bar attachment points. Lights have wire-mesh guards. Toolbox mounting places one light down low.

Keep up — to date

Keep up to date on the current off-road happenings by subscribing to the magazines and papers which specialize in reporting on this fast-growing sport. Here are some of the titles which are available and addresses of where you can subscribe. Firms who are catering to off-road enthusiasts regularly advertise their wares — tires, chassis, bodies, engines and so forth — in these periodicals. If you'd like a sample copy of one which is not available on your local newstand, send the single-copy price to the address shown and you'll get one by return mail.

Still other general-interest magazines and newspapers also carry news of off-road developments. Autoweek, Car Craft, Hot Rod, Popular Hotrodding, and Rod & Custom are a few of those whose editors work to keep their readers abreast of off roading, both in regular issues and in special, or yearbook issues.

Dune Buggies & Hot VW's
P.O. Box 2260
Costa Mesa, CA 92626
$1.00 sample copy
6 X year $6.00

Off-Road Vehicles
131 S. Barrington Place
Los Angeles, CA 90049
75¢ sample copy

4 X 4 & Dune Buggy News
Box 5547
Mission Hills, CA 91340
25¢ sample copy
$2.00 year

Double roll-bars on front and back buggies offer best protection if there's a rollover. Center car has single, well-braced bar. All drivers are shoulder-harnessed.

A sturdy roll-bar or roll-cage structure should be as much a part of every off-road machine as four good tires and wheels. The more experience one gains driving off the road, the more he realizes how very easily a vehicle can be placed on its side or upside down. With a sturdy roll-cage or roll-bar, this is usually of little consequence. Without such a structure--we won't go into all of the gory details.

There are no "tricks" or mysteries about these lifesaving structures--just good common sense. We never cease to be amazed at the lack of that commodity. Let's construct a basic roll bar for a glass-bodied buggy and a sedan--and then add to it to make a full cage.

On the glass car, you should locate the roll bar's bottom ends on pieces of flat steel plate. These should be in the neighborhood of four inches by six inches, at least 1/8-inch thick or heavier. While you're griping about the cost of living, better round up enough steel for two additional plates because we want to sandwich the floor pan

with them. In other words, two of them are welded to the roll-bar ends and the other two are placed on the underside of the floor pan. Upper and lower plates should be attached to the floor pan with no less than four, and preferably six, aircraft-quality 1/2-inch bolts snugged down on large washers on either end. Use castellated or self-locking nuts. Thus we have a sandwiched pan. The idea is to distribute load and keep everything in place when all that sudden loading on the roll-bar starts.

Radius the corners and edges of these plates or they will cut through the floor pan like a can opener when the roll bar is subjected to a sudden blow.

Johnny Johnson's Crown Manufacturing Special has a roll cage which is triangularly braced to shock towers at front and to engine mount at back. Bottom photos were made at impound area in Ensenada prior to start of 69 Baja 1000. By this time, car had three shocks on each rear wheel. Skid plate protects entire underside of engine and transmission. Cleaner atop cage is away from the dust storm churned up by those big rear tires.

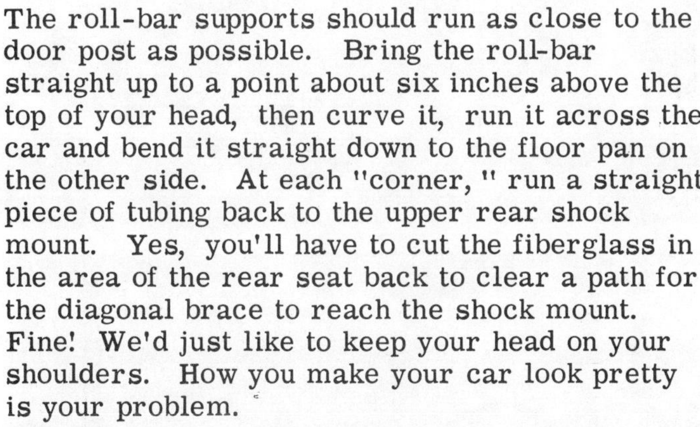

Fine example of well-built roll-cage or sedan. Note horizontals extending to front. Padding is taped to bars in the area of occupants' heads. That's a tractor-type air cleaner just below the rear window. Above photo of roll-bar installation shows typical shoulder-strap mounts.

The roll-bar supports should run as close to the door post as possible. Bring the roll-bar straight up to a point about six inches above the top of your head, then curve it, run it across the car and bend it straight down to the floor pan on the other side. At each "corner," run a straight piece of tubing back to the upper rear shock mount. Yes, you'll have to cut the fiberglass in the area of the rear seat back to clear a path for the diagonal brace to reach the shock mount. Fine! We'd just like to keep your head on your shoulders. How you make your car look pretty is your problem.

Two diagonals must be welded, each attaching to the top of the roll-bar at one end and to the top of the shock mount at the other end.

Run a straight piece of tubing from one side of the roll-bar to the other, just below shoulder height. This bar laterally strengthens the roll-bar structure, and becomes a shoulder-harness mounting.

Ray Longanecker of Say Ray Foreign Auto in Palo Alto, California points out that most dune-bug and sedan enthusiasts overlook the fact that the torsion bar tube and the center tunnel are the strongest points in the VW floor-pan-type chassis. He mounts roll bars on a saddle clamp made from a split piece of pipe. This pipe is curved to fit atop the torsion tube. Tubes for clamping bolts are welded onto each side of the split pipe to permit clamping the mount to the torsion tube. Then he brings a diagonal support forward from the top center of the roll bar, terminating this in a sturdy plate which is shaped to fit over the tunnel and welded or bolted into place. Ray also suggests that this locates the roll bar just perfectly for a buggy with a shortened floor pan, and really does not place the bar too far back of you, even in a sedan, most especially if you are building a roll cage as discussed in the following paragraph.

For a full roll-cage structure, the roll-bar we've just built stays the same. Another roll-bar loop is now bent to fit as closely as possible to the dash and door opening on a sedan. On a glass car, get this loop as close to the dash as possible. For sedans, a slight bend is often placed in the roll-bar in the area just below the dash to ease getting in and out of the car. The upper two bends of this bar should be connected with straight pieces that connect to the bends on the

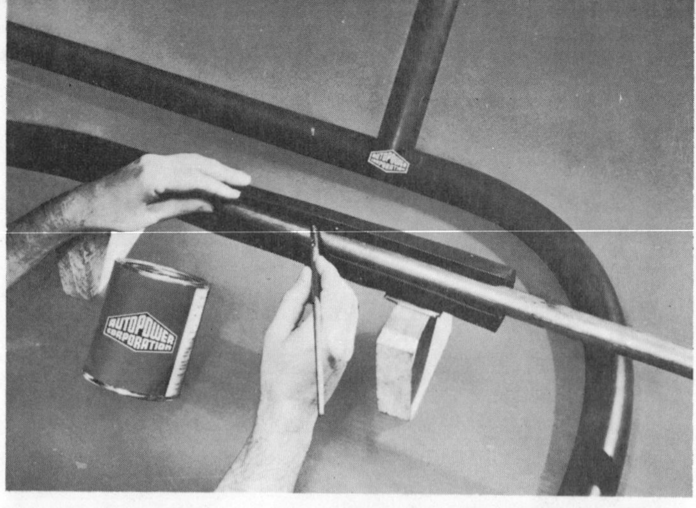

Excellent example of roll-bar/roll-cage mounting to VW floor pan includes hefty plate, and lock washers under the nuts. Bottom edges and corners of the plate should be rounded so they won't shear the floor when given a sudden sharp blow.

Covering roll-bar and roll-cage tubes with insulation rubber prevents damage to occupants.

Accompanying photos show how the roll-bar can be tied into the engine support at rear. Although the four photos are all of Corvairs, it is generally agreed that the VW and Porsche also need a rear engine mount for serious off-road work.

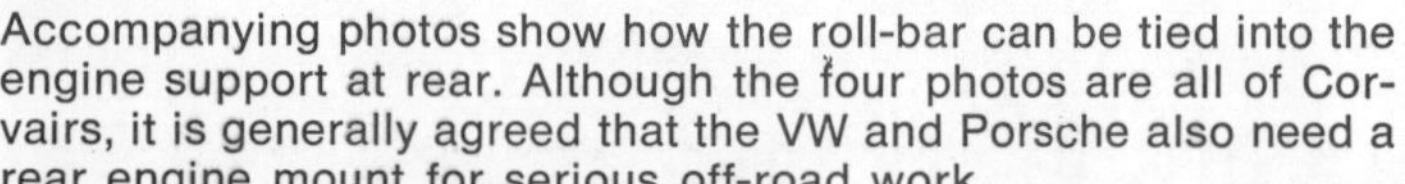

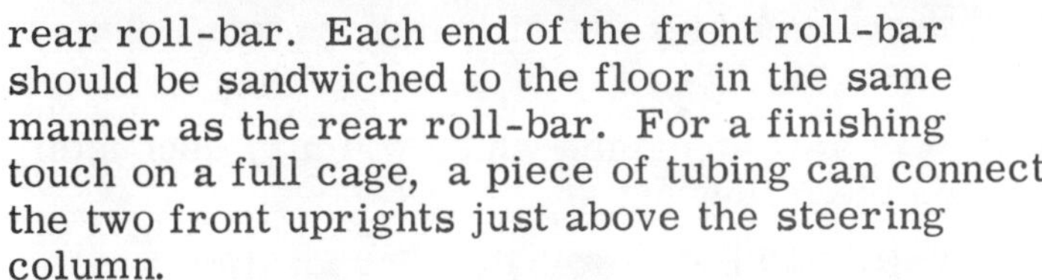

Two sand buggies show how the ideal mounting/strength points can be used: torsion bar tube at back and tunnel at front. Most glass-bodied cars can also use these same mounting points.

rear roll-bar. Each end of the front roll-bar should be sandwiched to the floor in the same manner as the rear roll-bar. For a finishing touch on a full cage, a piece of tubing can connect the two front uprights just above the steering column.

Such a structure in either a sedan or glass car will withstand a tremendous amount of punishment. Neat. How do we build it? There are several ways. Assuming you can find a heads-up race car shop in your area, you can turn the job over to them. Or, you can shop for a competent metal-fabricating shop and dictate what you have in mind. You can do it yourself, assuming that you are a very good welder and can measure accurately. Round tubing MUST always be used for a roll-bar or roll structure. Most racing associations plainly state square tubing shall not be used in any roll-bar or roll-cage structures. The reason for this is that round tubing has greater torsional, tensional and compressive strength than square tubing of comparable size. Because your life depends on the strength of this structure, use the strongest stuff available. Something on the order of 1-1/2-inch-diameter mild steel, 0.095-inch wall (13-gauge) is sufficiently strong for a lightweight car such as a VW-based sedan or buggy. For heavier vehicles, 2-inch, 0.120-inch wall (11-gauge) is standard.

The ends of the tubing to be welded to adjoining tubes should be trimmed to a "fish-mouth" shape on a band saw, with hand shears, in an end mill or with a hole saw chucked in a drill press to ensure a close, tight fit. With some practice, and a good breakfast, you can trim the 0.090-inch wall stuff with left and right hand shears. Heavier wall tubing must be cut with a machine. This fitting of tubes where they join is the second MUST in building a roll-bar/roll-cage. The first was the use of round tubing, remember? Trim the ends so that they fit flush with the adjoining tubing.

The third MUST is too often violated without regard for the consequences. Regard each weld as if your life depended on it, because it does. If you cannot weld a workmanlike bead, forget this job. A roll-cage may be arced, short arced, heli-arced or gas welded. The method used is far less important than the ultimate quality (strength) of the joint.

The big drawback in constructing a roll-bar is bending the tubing. Most large metropolitan areas have at least one metal fabricating shop with a mandrel bender. These large, hydraulically actuated machines will bend tubing without changing tube diameter at any point. If possible, find one of these machines (not to buy--they cost thousands), explain what you are building, what

In case of a roll over, this is a shaky setup. Roll bar is high enough to protect driver and passenger in a slow roll over, but lacks correct bracing for off-road racing. A roll cage is preferable. Those wheels on the rear would be fine in the sand. In rock, you'd soon be looking for a hammer because the tire sidewall must extend past the outer edge of the rim to protect the wheel itself from damage. Car is a "Grasshopper."

This fiberglas copy of a Model T roadster body is a clever and rather practical approach to off roading with a different look. Vehicle may be driven on the street. Luggage rack can be stacked with gear, spare tire gives good protection in case something is rammed at speed and fenders go a long way to keep the vehicle relatively clean. When the monsoon hits, that little top isn't for sale! Neat roll bar behind cab needs added bracing. This is another version of the "Grasshopper."

wall thickness and what diameter. With stiff wire, fabricate a pattern of what you want bent and let the shop do the job. . . after you have a quoted price for the work.

In case you happen to live in East Overshoe, Nowhere, and locating a mandrel bender is impossible, you can bend the tube yourself. This will take a while, but things are probably slow in East Overshoe anyway. Buy a length of steel tubing long enough to shape a roll-bar. We won't buy any pieced-together roll-bars! Weld or braze a cap over one end of the tubing. Automotive freeze plugs (brass) are just the ticket for this. Now pack (and we do mean pack) the entire length of tubing with sand. Heat the area to be bent with a gas torch, and then slowly pull the tubing around to the correct bend. You'll need a couple of healthy friends for this or a large vise and some work area. Saw the ends off the tube, poke the sand out and finish building the roll-cage. Don't scoff at this--lots of roll-bars and lots of headers have been built this way.

In a sedan, make sure you leave enough room between the roll-bars and the roof to get a torch or electrode to the joints for the diagonals.

The most common way of finishing off a roll-bar or roll-cage is to cover all the tubing with foam rubber. The trick here is to visit a commercial air conditioning firm and buy the foam insulation which is placed around the pipes leading from the compressor to the evaporator. This tubing comes in long lengths (six feet is standard) and in a wide variety of internal diameters and thicknesses. If you plan ahead, some sections of this tubing may be put into place on the structure before it is completed, if you want to go to the extra trouble of wrapping those pieces in the

area of a weld with asbestos to prevent a fire. If not, just split the insulation with a razor blade, coat the inside with contact cement and glue it around the roll-bars. The material is a closed cell Neoprene which is impervious to gasoline, oil and water. Many off-roaders then wrap this with cloth-backed duct tape. This tape is manufactured by several firms (3M, for instance) and is available from firms which install heating and air-conditioning systems. This is not necessary.

Some of the tradenames which you may encounter include the following:

RUBATEX by Rubatex Corporation

ARMAFLEX by Armstrong

AEROTUBE by Johns-Manville

All are equally usable for roll-bar wrapping and for cushioning other items in the cockpit, such as steering-brake levers, side tubes, gearshift levers, etc.

While you are laying out the coins for this foam tubing, buy an extra four to six feet. Plan on shoving about a foot over each strap of the shoulder harness in the area that passes over your shoulders. This padding keeps the straps from cutting into your shoulders. Depending on the type of shoulder harness end, you may be able to get the tubing over the straps without splitting the tubing. Split or unsplit, tape can be used to keep the tubing in place on the straps.

We'll not state uncategorically that you must have seat belts and shoulder harness to drive off the road. We are not normally concerned with high-speed collisions or roll overs, but consider the great amount of vehicle movement involved. In desert terrain at even moderate speed, the vehicle will pitch, yaw, drop straight down and then slam vertically several times a minute. After half an hour of this without seat belts and shoulder harness, most people feel as if they just stepped out of a washing machine. The treatment is roughly akin to drinking a quart of water and then attempting to run a mile or two. Seat belts and shoulder harness will snug an occupant down in the seat and prevent movement. When movement is limited then your chances of getting hurt are minimized. Without a seat belt or shoulder harness, you'll find it a relatively simple matter to knock yourself colder than a mackerel against a sedan roof or a glass car's roll-bar. Typical times when this can occur happen when the vehicle drops down and to one side at about the same time. While you are thinking about driver/passenger movement within the vehicle, keep in mind that it takes no small amount of practice to be able to drink from a canteen in an off-road race car without drenching yourself or chipping a couple of teeth. That's why you'll often see the canteen strapped down and a long plastic hose used for a straw. Seat belts and shoulder harness are beginning to sound pretty good, aren't they?

Incidentally, soft-plastic containers — such as bleach bottles and some canteens -- are easy to fit into some out of the way place in your car. Attention to this bit of detail costs less than repairing chipped or broken teeth — and it's a long way to the dentist or a pain pill when you're out in the middle of the desert — or half way down Baja.

Water pipe, threaded fittings, square tubing, crimped bends, bends of more than 90 degrees, no diagonal supports, bad welding, an insufficient mounting area on the floor pan are all easy ways to spot a poorly constructed roll-bar structure. Avoid all these pitfalls like the plague whether you are building, buying, driving or riding.

Those enthusiasts who run in the desert almost never need to be reminded that a good roll-bar or cage is one way to ensure long life. Sand dune addicts are somewhat harder to convince. From time to time we read of some of them in the accident or obituary columns. Some sort of roll-cage or roof-type structure is essential for running safely in the sand, because a single roll-bar can easily sink farther into a sand dune than the height of the driver's head--another quick way to collect one or more broken necks.

Even though you know that you are well protected with a roll bar or a roll cage, it is prudent to drive as if these protective devices were not there. Why? Because a roll bar/cage will not protect you and your passenger from all of the injury-producing situations which can occur when you get upside down. It is always possible to get a hand under the edge of the windshield or the side of the body as you roll over, or worse yet, if you are not wearing a shoulder harness, your head can take quite a beating under some circumstances. Some drivers get the protection installed and then drive as if these devices were some kind of a "magic shield" against all injury or harm. Ain't so--there's no way that you can protect yourself from all possible injury-producing situations off road--unless your vehicle is a war surplus tank--and even then there would be some way that you could get hurt. Care and caution in approaching the off-road driving/racing situation is always demanded.

Roll bar is an integral part of the Deserter GS tubular space frame, shown here with fiberglas floor pan installed. Suspension for this mid-engined buggy is stock VW at front. Coil spring over shock is used at the rear with swing axles. Brakes can be Porsche or VW drum or disc.

Mid-engined Deserter GS with engine cover removed to show Corvair 140HP engine with Holley four barrel. Engine is Crown-adapted to VW transaxle. Six Dzus fasteners attach fiberglas engine cover.

Skid Plates
What's the skinny?

A good skidplate: braced at the top to prevent its crumpling backward under loading, extends up far enough for protection. It can also serve as a bumper for pushing another vehicle.

Like everything else on an off-road machine, the skid plate arrangement should be a common-sense product. For a vehicle used only on the sand dunes, a skid plate is necessary only if you plan to do wheelies or wheel stands so that the back edge of the engine touches the ground. This is highly unlikely on sedans and glass-bodied cars of conventional layout and design. The problem can be neatly solved on a super-light rail dragster by fabricating two pieces of tail-pipe stock into a skid extending from the trans-axle mounting yoke bolts to the backside of the engine and curving up to a vertical attitude at the rear. How you keep all the exhaust piping up and out of the way is your problem.

Sand machines need light-weight skid plates for actually skidding the car out of impossible situations.

This is in sharp contrast with the amount of protection required for the underside of the engine and transaxle of a vehicle to be run through rock. It does not take a very large rock to rip open a valve cover or bend it badly enough to leak. Even smaller rocks, or even sticks, can seriously damage a pushrod tube. In the desert areas of the Western United States, you'll encounter more than just a few rocks large and hard enough to disembowel a transaxle or engine.

So, let's build a skid plate. There are several on the market; many are custom-fabricated in dune-buggy shops and the job is a simple one for any metal-fabricating shop. We say this because few of us are blessed with the equipment to do the job correctly. And, like the roll-bar -- this must be done right to eliminate long, un-scheduled walks.

Begin the skid plate at the rear torsion tube to protect the transaxle "nose." Extend this part of the plate the width and length of the transaxle-mounting yoke. Sedans or glass cars not to be used in competition off the road can use a large barn-door hinge under the torsion-tube center so the transaxle skid plate can fold down. Weld the hinge to the underside of the floorpan where it joins the torsion tube, then drill the leading edge of the skid plate so that it can be bolted to the trailing wing of the hinge. This makes removal of the entire plate easy. The plate may be constructed of 3/16-inch mild steel or aluminum to save weight. If made of aluminum, the plate should be at least 6061-T6 quality material. Weld tabs to the sides or bottom of the yoke at the rear to secure the plate to brackets securely mounted to the chassis. Thus, to service the transaxle, unbolt two or more bolts at the rear and the plate hinges down while remaining attached to the front.

Drill a number of holes throughout the plate to let liquids drain out. These should not be larger than 1/2-inch. At low speed, a rock or stump can hang a vehicle up on a larger skid-plate hole. The vehicle usually rides up on the obstruction and then stops with much of the weight lifted off the rear wheels--which means no traction. This can be a lot of fun. Experience speaks.

The engine skid plate may be a part of the transaxle skid plate. It may hinge from the transaxle skid plate or it may be a rigid, separate structure. On a sedan, pieces of angle iron can be extended downward from the engine-compartment side of the inner fender and used as rear mount brackets for the plate which should always extend several inches past the crankshaft pulley. Re-

Those rocks get downright unfriendly, not to mention destructive, when you bang down on them. Here a well skid-plated FUNCO Wampuskitty shows its stuff in a Southern California dry river bed.

member to extend the plate past the valve covers and lip the leading edge upward so that the plate will ride over any obstruction. Spend some time under your car with paper, pencil and steel rule and sketch out an effective plate. Then you can have a sheet metal shop do the shearing and braking for a minimum outlay. As with the transaxle plate, drill 1/2-inch holes at random in the engine skid plate. Either plan on pulling the engine for each oil change or cut a somewhat larger hole under the drain plug. We are not being facetious about pulling the engine for an oil change. If you are setting up a vehicle for competition, great is the fear that a rock jammed in the hole at speed will crack the case open. Leave small holes in the plate or fabricate a plate cover for the drain hole.

Just below the oil pump, on the underside of the VW engine case, there is a small tab. Because there is a hole in the tab, some off-roaders think that this is a dandy place to secure the rear of the engine skid plate. This is another bad idea, so forget we ever mentioned it! The skid plate's purpose is to deflect or absorb energy--NOT TO PASS IT ON to the very component you're trying to protect. There should be a minimum of one-inch clearance between any point on the case bottom and the skid plate. Ensure that you keep this one-inch clearance by building a one-inch-square steel tube into your skid plate or welding this tube onto the transaxle cradle mount immediately below the frame-yoke ends. Let the skid plate get gouged, buckled or bent--but don't ever let it contact the engine. Avoid any temptation to attach the rear of the plate to the engine. A sharp upward blow to the rear of the engine usually results in a broken transmission nose (now you know what caused that last broken nose).

Just below the oil pump, on the underside of the VW engine case, there is a small tab. Because there is a hole in the tab, some off-roaders think that this is a dandy place to secure the rear of the engine skid plate. This is another bad idea, so forget we ever mentioned it! The skid plate's purpose is to deflect or absorb energy--NOT TO PASS IT ON to the very component you're trying to protect. There should be a minimum of one-inch clearance between any point on the case bottom and the skid plate. Let the plate get gouged, buckled or bent--but don't let it contact the engine.

As in the case of the transaxle skid plate, the engine plate may be fashioned from steel or aluminum.

Depending on your talents and tools, 1/2-inch plywood can be used to construct a very durable, low-cost skid plate. These are most often one-piece units shaped as a fat "T," with the leg of the T covering the transaxle all the way to the torsion tube. The two arms extend past the front, back and outside edges of the valve covers. The steel tube which you have welded onto the outside edges of the transaxle cradle mount can be drilled to permit attaching the plywood with carriage bolts. At the rear of a sedan, angle steel extended downward from the inner fender panels can serve as mounts. On a glass car this is more difficult, and a metal structure must be fabricated from the rear shock mounts, downward and under the rear of the engine. If this must be done, then you will probably be better off by making the plate out of metal.

Two views of transaxle/engine skid plate combination used on a FUNCO factory-prepared Wampuskitty off-road racer. Transaxle skid plate is bent from 3/16-inch steel and fits along entire length of yoke extending back from VW torsion-tube assembly. Skid plate nose is bent upward so debris cannot enter to jam between the plate and transaxle housing. Welding skid plate to yoke is not recommended because of the extreme difficulty in getting to the two front mounting capscrews. Angled pieces welded to the bottom stiffen the plate, provide a "runner" and add even further protection against gouging by rocks. These angles extend onto the engine skid plate which is also bent from 3/16-inch steel and welded to the transaxle plate. Turned up leading edge deflects rocks and brush downward. Plate extends past valve cover outer edge at each side.

Here's one you can learn from — check that flat aluminum skidplate bolted to the straight tubing runners with carriage bolts to eliminate snagging. Plate extends to protect the valve covers; back to guard against tearing off exhaust system. Rear cage structure is for short-course racing, but couldn't be too far wrong for back-woods running. Before going too far on a project such as this, make sure the engine can easily be removed. Cable attached to the frame (arrow) also attaches to the swing axle, serving as a bottoming device to save the shock should torsion-arm stop get beaten away.

Skid plate is sturdily made but fails the ultimate test because it does not extend past the edges of the rocker arm covers. These are modified Terra tires — too aggressive for sand, except for an extremely light vehicle. Tread pattern has been modified to reduce bite. Shadow reveals holes in plate.

Ribs of angle iron on the upper side of the skid plate add strength and prevent plate flexing when hit hard. Metal mesh and strap surround generator belt and keep fingers away from pulley and belt. Accessory oil filter sticks through mesh.

Porsche engine is not generally used for off-roading because of high price and lack of low-RPM torque — but there are exceptions. Skid plate was fabricated from leaf springs from an old car during "pit stop" in long-distance race after another skid plate was torn off.

When building a complete cage around the rear of a buggy which is a part of the skid plate, leave sufficient room to pull the engine rearward when removing it. Wire-mesh storage rack is hinged at the rear and secured at front with Jeep hood latches for access to engine.

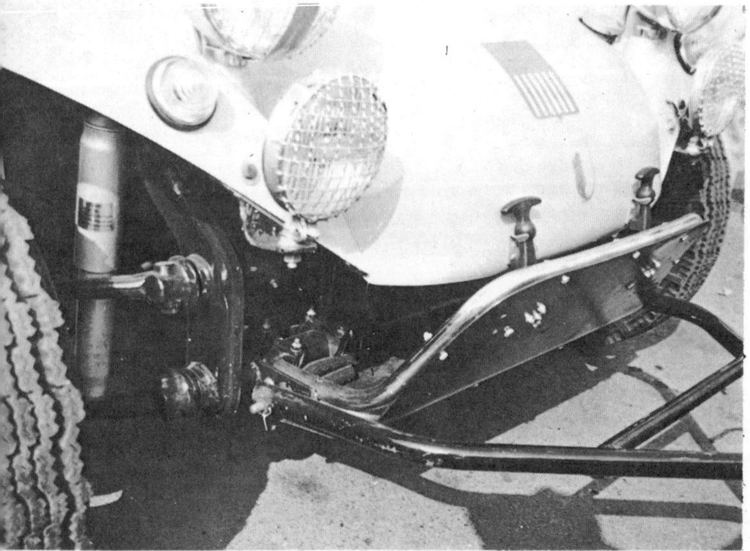

Combination skid plate/bumper arrangement for glass car front is a good move because nosing into a bank or rock can crack the hood all the way to the cowl. Repairs of such magnitude are expensive. Space front skid plate away from the fiberglass.

Exhaust pipe flanges (arrows) may be used with round tubing to achieve a nerf-bar arrangement which unbolts for engine work. Underside of nerf bars support skid plate.

Top: Sandbug's well designed skidder protects underside, curves up at back. Center: Bandido with flat engine has skid plate with angle runners underneath. Plate should extend farther toward sides to protect valve covers, even if heavy aluminum type is used. Bottom: Serious Baja competitor's skid plate is braced, but needs a piece of rubber pad between plate and engine to soften the really hard blows.

Top: Lots of room between this plate and the engine. Front and side bends stiffen plate. High exhaust is out of the way. Center: Basket-style rear wraparound directs skid-plate shocks into Bandido's frame. Engine rear motor mount can attach to this structure. Bottom: Flat plate has hard rubber (or tire section) under engine case to soften blows. Bends in plate would stiffen it. Front should have bent-up lip to keep rocks out of area between plate and engine.

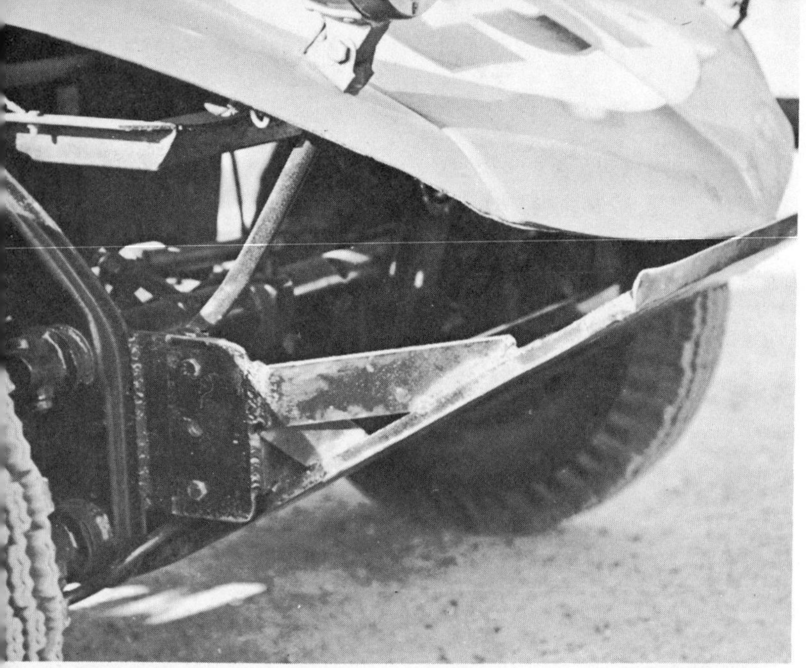

Five more photos of front skid plates, ranging from home-made buggies, through sedans and even including a bus! Most tie into the front-suspension cross tube and extend back to the body structure so that rocks will have a harder time finding a place to hang onto — thus helping you to keep going. Most of these angle upward in the front, and the sharper ramp angle of the top left plate is possibly most effective.

Face of the competition. The extreme light weight of a trail-rigged bike makes this vehicle hard to beat in long-distance off-road events. The largest bikes rigged for off-roading won't go over 350 pounds — as opposed to 1300 pounds for the average unloaded dune buggy or 1800 pounds for a sedan.

Whether you plan to go racing off-road — or just enjoy playing around in the boonies — the chances are great that you'll end up cheating yourself by making your buggy or sedan too heavy. And, you'll probably overload it with too much in the way of food, camping gear, spare parts, tools and tires. Because the overall performance of your vehicle is directly related to engine power and total weight (loaded and wet), the car will not perform as you'd like it to — and you will be to blame.

A strange thing occurs when the average off-road enthusiast realizes that he has four wheels and an engine to carry his junk. He begins to make vast lists of the food and personal-comfort items which can somehow be jammed into the confines of a buggy or sedan. Then, he adds on all of the parts that could possibly break (forgetting that some parts could not be replaced in time to finish a race). Hugh amounts of oil and gas and water — and — and — and — the list grows and grows. When the car starts out, it's sometimes hard to see the driver and passenger because the gear that's stuffed all around them practically hides them from view. Now, it's bad enough to start

across town with a car loaded like that — but it is literally ridiculous to do so on an off-road trip, regardless of whether you are racing or off on a fun excursion.

By contrast, watch the motorcycle riders come to the starting line. There's nothing hung onto those men or machines that is not absolutely essential. No spare parts to speak of, little food and drink, and no spare clothes, sleeping bags or jugs of wine. Why? Well, in the first place, there's no way to carry all of the extra and unneeded stuff. Secondly, the bike rider has probably done a far better job of planning his parts supply, tire replacements and food stops. Thirdly, every bike rider knows how unwieldy his steed would become when piled high and loaded down.

The car driver, on the other hand, equips himself as a rolling auto parts house, garage, machine shop, grocery store, bar and hotel — and the result is predictable. The car usually fails to make it to the first check point, or drops by the wayside not much farther down the course. Tires, shocks and suspension components all take an extra beating from the weight. The car's performance is much less than it could and should be.

Handling becomes evil and wears out the driver — and worries the passenger — as the unwieldy car wallows like a sled over tough terrain that absolutely demands nimbleness.

What's the answer? GO LIGHT. Start thinking like a bike rider or back packer. Experienced back packers walk where they go. You can be sure that they don't take unnecessary things with them — at least not after the first time. Read. Buy or borrow these two books and learn the joy of equipping yourself with the minimum amount of things — which have an uncanny knack for getting in the way of having fun.

THE COMPLETE WALKER (The joys and techniques of hiking and backpacking), by Colin Fletcher. Published by A. A. Knopf, 1969.

GOING LIGHT WITH BACKPACK OR BURRO, by David Brower. Published by the Sierra Club.

Sharp observers of the racing scene will have noted by now that there are quite a few single-seater buggies racing these days. Baja rules, at least through 1969's race, permitted a single driver with no passenger requirement. Thus, the vehicle weight can be kept down (in the case of a buggy or sedan), and both drivers can start out completely fresh.

This means that you do not need the extra seat, nor the food, water and duffle for a second person. After all, you wouldn't think of strapping in weight equivalent to that of a passenger. And, if you know the course and trust your own navigational ability, there are few situations where the passenger does much more than get scared or get in the way. There's another plus benefit which may not be obvious. Pre-running a race course, such as Baja, takes a lot of time and a great amount of concentration and note-taking. If you split the chore, then each driver has to learn only half of the course — and that is a lot easier job.

Compare and then think about how you can lighten the load your buggy or sedan is carrying. Top photo shows heavily loaded buggy at start of '69 Baja 1000. Tires and duffle stacked way high have put about 400 pounds where it can only raise the center of gravity. Inside of car was similarly loaded. Car did not finish because of suspension failure. Bottom photo shows competitors finishing at La Paz in a Bandido which they dieted by constructing most of the body from canvas snapped to steel-tube chassis. Spare tire on top is just that — spare: narrow rim and narrow tire is to get the crew home, not to race on. That's a 30-pound saving (or more) right there.

Below: Hurst's VW shifter selects reverse by pulling up spring-loaded trigger. Holding trigger up locks out 3rd and 4th and creates straight-line reverse-to-first shifting for rocking out of sand, mud or snow easily. Should be part of every bug or buggy.

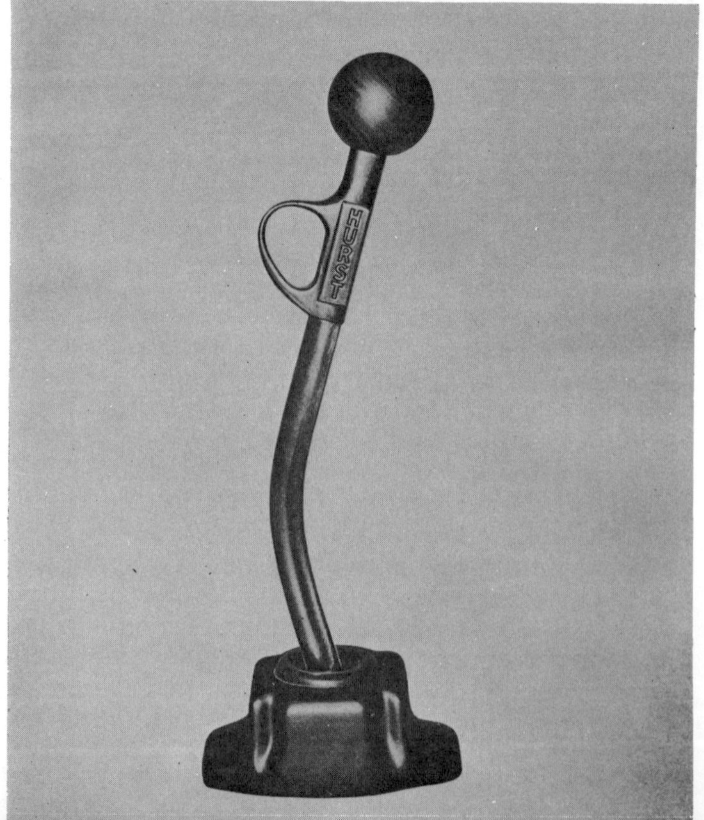

To get this sort of action, you need a lot of power or a light car.
In either case, frame and suspension loadings soar. If the equipment is not up to it, chronic failures result.

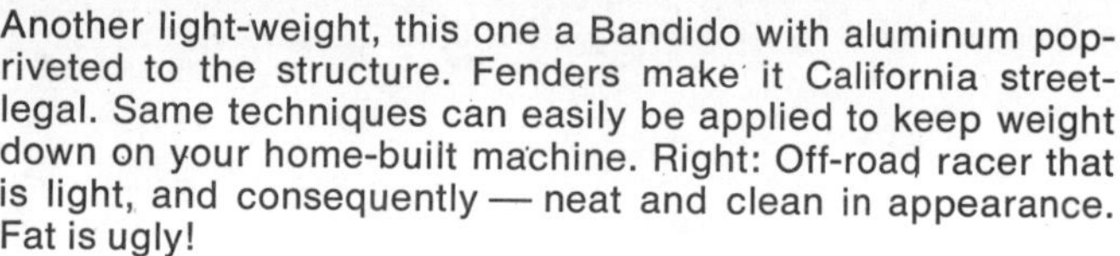

Another light-weight, this one a Bandido with aluminum pop-riveted to the structure. Fenders make it California street-legal. Same techniques can easily be applied to keep weight down on your home-built machine. Right: Off-road racer that is light, and consequently — neat and clean in appearance. Fat is ugly!

Continuing the light-weight theme, here's a perfect example. Tube-steel frame and basically stock engines can get you places the rest of the crowd can't go. Because of light weight, flotation and traction requirements drop. Tires shown are recapped street tires. Left: A heavy vehicle such as the famous Baja Boot, puts a horrendous strain on frame and suspension members. Although heavy vehicles can be quite competitive, a different driving technique is called for to keep the vehicles together.

It had to come to this. The need for light weight and the trend to single seaters caused Funco to introduce the Super Single at the 1969 Bug-In 3. A full roll cage is a part of the mild-steel chassis. Brackets and mounts accept VW components — front-end, and either swing axle or four-joint transaxle. Only the steering and shifter components are special. Wheelbase is 88 inches and height as shown is 42 inches.

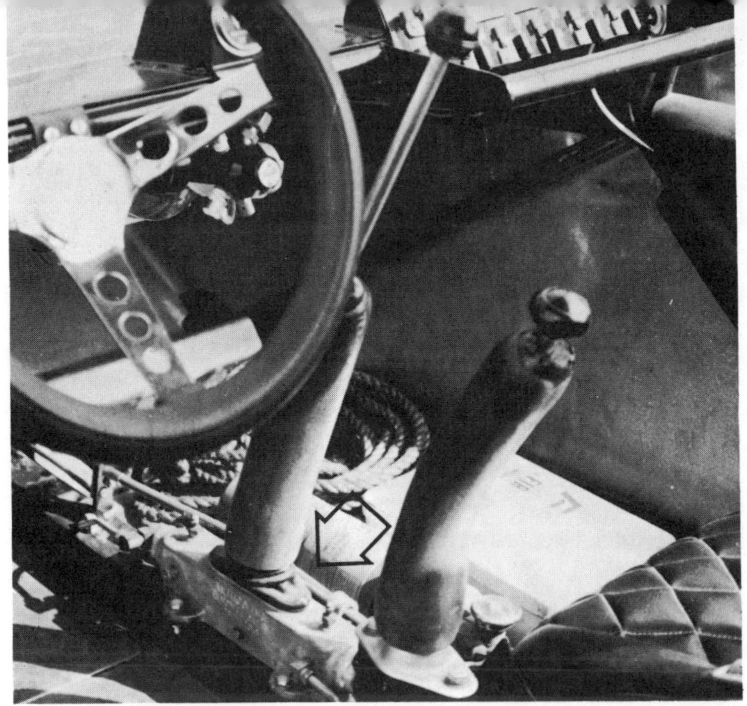

Steering Brakes

Steering brake installed in Baja racer. Unit shown is an Almico which costs about $70. Note that steering brake lever and gearshift lever are both covered with insulation rubber. One off-road ride will convince you of the need for such details.

Why didn't the car go where I aimed it when I came off the top of that last dune? The same thing happened on that silty road at speed the other day, but then I clobbered a rock and the day's fun was over. Took awhile to fix the damages, too. Lots of off roaders, especially those with light, short wheelbase cars, have found that the front wheels by themselves no longer provide adequate directional control. There is a way around the problem. Steer with the rear wheels. How? Easy! If you brake one rear wheel, the other rear wheel will cause the car to pivot around the braked wheel. Brake the left rear wheel and the car turns left — just like a farm tractor or a tracked vehicle.

Here again, the parts manufacturers have put kits together so that the solution becomes a bolt-on. There are at least three different manufacturers of steering brakes, and two types of these brakes. One uses the stock VW emergency-brake set up and allows you to brake either rear wheel with the single emergency shoe. That's Crown Manufacturing's contribution. It uses two brake levers, one for each direction. Two others, Almico, Inc. and Meisman Brake Control, make hydraulic models which lock up both shoes of either rear wheel. These offer identical performance, permitting normal service-brake and emergency-brake operation, whether or not the steering brake is being used. That is, you could be turning with the steering brake and have to make a panic stop. The regular brake system will function normally. These units also function as a hill holder when you have to get going again on a hill. That task becomes a lot easier because you can hold the car in place with the steering brake while you keep one foot on the clutch and the other on the throttle — with no need for wild stabs at one or the other — with the possibility of killing the engine. . . . . or rolling backwards over a cliff.

The usual instructions supplied with the steering brakes show a hook up which steers the car to the right when you push forward on the brake-control lever, and left when you pull it back. Some off-roaders reverse the hook up to get what seems to them to be a more natural operation when compared with turning the steering wheel. Thus, they prefer to push forward to go left, just as they would push up with the right hand. Pull back to go right, as in pulling the wteering wheel toward you. Regardless of how you prefer to hook up a steering brake, it's an important addition for your machine.

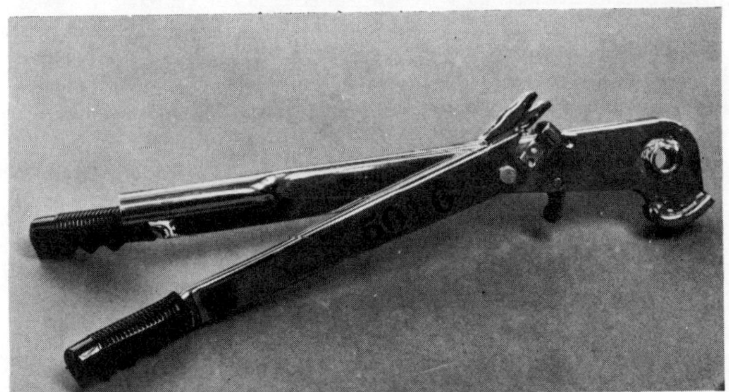

Crown's Select-A-Traction cable-actuated steering brake. Mounts in place of regular emergency brake. Center handle serves as emergency brake because it can tension both cables. Other handles control one brake each, thus either rear wheel can be stopped while power is applied to the other for exciting turns in the dirt!

The two hydraulic types both install in about the same way. Left and right rear brake lines are separated at the T-joint and reconnected to the appropriate pressure outlets on the steering-brake cylinder assembly. The main brake line to the T-fitting is attached to the front of the Almico unit, or to the center port of the Meismann affair.

If you use the emergency-brake type steering set up, then you will want to be sure to clean out every last trace of oil and grease from the cable housing. Otherwise, you will probably find that the sand will find its way into the cables and make them difficult or impossible to operate.

There's still another brake-system modification that you may want to include when preparing your off-road machine. That's a front-brake-lockout device. Several are available. The simplest way is to install a valve to the front brakes. Turning the valve OFF disables the front brakes. Special valves are sold for the purpose. They have to withstand the pressures developed in the brake system, of course. Almico has an electrically operated valve that lets you eliminate front-brake action at any time by switching a dash-mounted toggle switch to the SAND position. You get all brakes back into operation by switching back to ROAD.

Why lockout the front brakes? Why do some sand buggy builders leave front brakes off of their cars? In sandy going, especially downhill, use of the front brakes causes plowing or dipping. With all brakes working, an attempt to stop may cause the front wheels to dig in — and the back comes around to try to pass the front end. If you

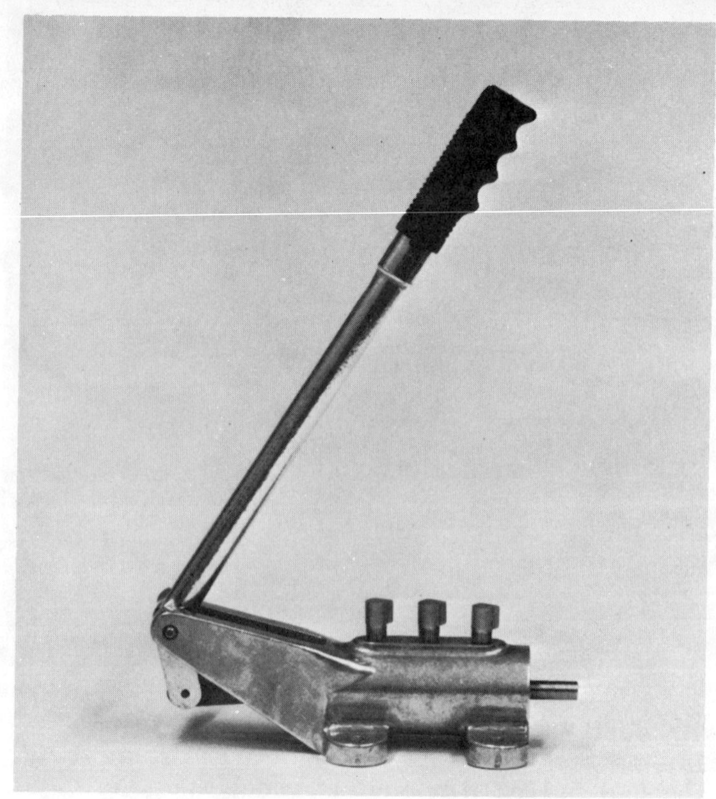

The Meisman Hydraulic Brake Control can be spliced into the stock brake set up to provide positive braking of either rear wheel for good directional control in the dirt. Costs about $40.

are thus starting to "cross up," you may be able to recover by letting up on the brakes long enough for the front wheels to climb on top of the sand again. Without front wheel brakes, or with them inoperative, only the rear tires dig in, slowing the machine in a straight line without loss of control.

MEISMAN BRAKE CONTROL INSTALLED

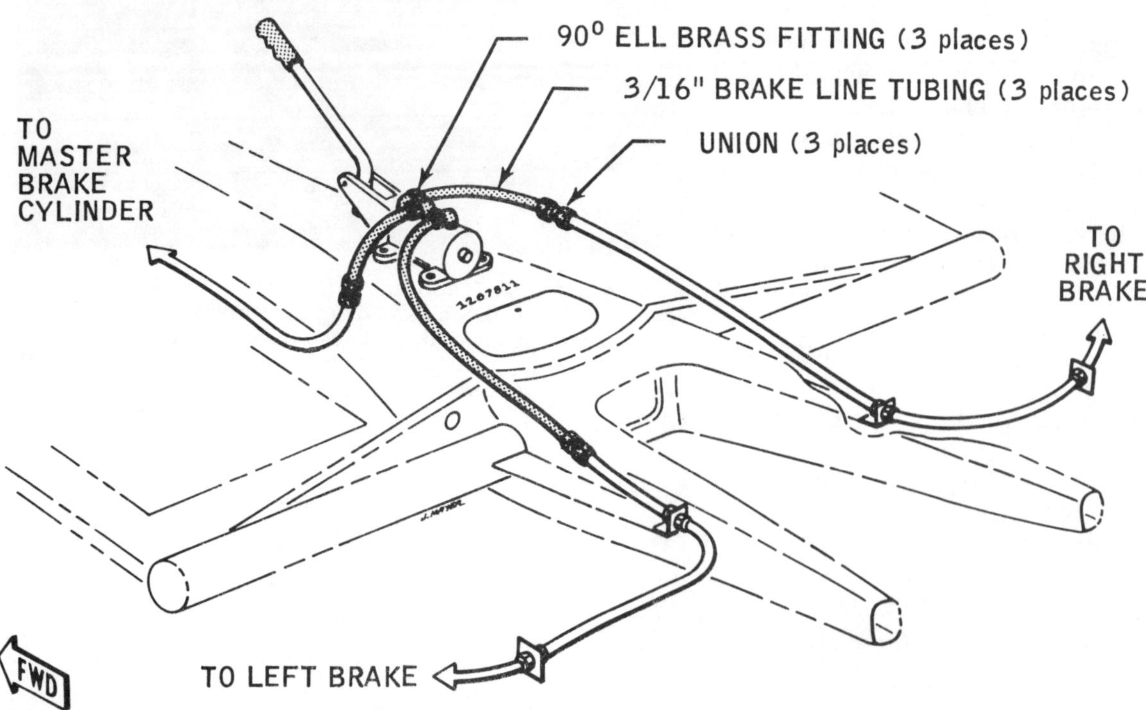

Here's a slick dress-up item for a glass car: the gas-filler assembly from a 'Vette. There are several accessory caps similar to this and the late Dodge Charger also has a flush, hinged cap.

We can assume that Volkswagen designers never intended that the little sedan should be stripped of body, a section removed from the floor pan and the resulting chassis topped by a fragile, lightweight fiberglass body. We can assume this, and also that they didn't intend that this "creation" should be driven at speed down cow trails, open desert, plowed fields and rock-bottomed streams. The dune buggy as we know it does all of this and more rather well. But there are problems which crop up off the road which are never given any thought by a buggy owner who only drives on pavement.

The sedan body is, in large part, responsible for the VW floor pan's stiffness. Between the front and rear axles there is only one strong section. This is the pan-length hump or tunnel which contains the shifter mechanism, clutch and throttle cables, etc. Thus we expect one rather limited area to support a body, gas tank, battery, seats, people: all the things that fit between the front and rear wheels. This the tunnel does rather well. But floor pans have been known to begin flexing, then cracking and finally separating after being run hard off the road, even when used as originally intended with the sedan body intact.

We have no intent of going into all the steps necessary to construct a fiberglass-bodied dune buggy, but rather we would attempt to head off problems before they crop up if you are contemplating building such a vehicle to be used off road.

Several accessory manufacturers sell VW-floor pan-reinforcing kits. Basically, these kits consist of lengths of bent tubing which fit into the channel along the sides of the pan. Mild steel tubing--square or round--may easily be heated with a torch, bent to the correct shape (one bend per side) and dropped into the channel. This tubing should then be welded into place. From the underside of the pan, this tubing can be drilled to match the bolt pattern of the cut floor pan. Additional strength can be given the floor pan for a glass-bodied car if extra work is put into the body mounting. Wherever the body mounts to the pan, create a sandwich of light-gauge steel strips on top of the glass lip. Also, use large-diameter washers under all the mounting-bolt heads. Thus, the bolt passes through a large diameter washer, the steel strip, the fiberglass body lip and then into the metal floor.

Most builders attach the body to the floor pan with the same number of bolts as there are holes in the floor pan. This is not enough. Double up on the number of bolts. When snugging the body on for the last time, pull all the bolts down to about the same torque load--then go around the body again for a final tightening. Use Loctite on all of the bolts, too.

Most glass bodies have provisions for mounting the stock VW gas tank as it was mounted in the sedan: with small metal tabs which go around the seam/lip of the tank. For a glass car going off the road, additional tabs should be made up to eliminate the possibility of movement which can cause breakage and spillage. These tabs should be larger than the stock mountings to ensure against failures.

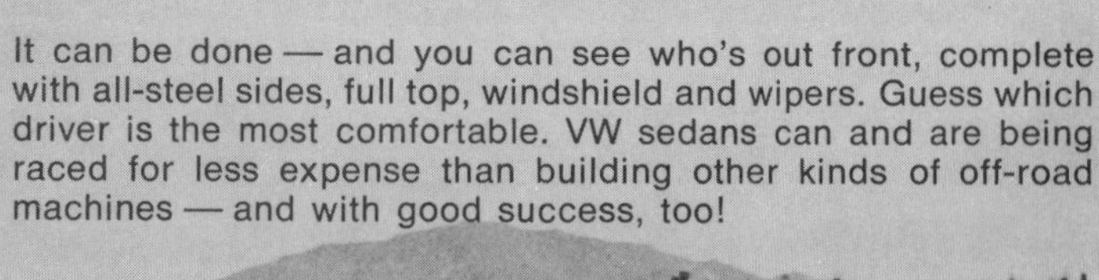

It can be done — and you can see who's out front, complete with all-steel sides, full top, windshield and wipers. Guess which driver is the most comfortable. VW sedans can and are being raced for less expense than building other kinds of off-road machines — and with good success, too!

Sedan Building

Yes, folks do race sedans in Baja. These were seen in the impound area at Ensenada for the start of the '69 Baja 1000.

With the running gear cared for as we've previously suggested, the steel-bodied sedan can be left just about like it is and driven off the road with only a few alterations. Or, it can be given the full "trick" treatment. We'll run down a list of some of the more sensible and popular things to do to a sedan. Your own budget and time allowance can dictate the finished product which you take off the road.

For sheer strength, the earlier the sedan the better. The reason for this is that heavier gauge metal and more of it was used in the early VW body. Doorposts and windshield posts were thicker and more metal (a lot more) was placed in the inner roof panel. Gradually, this metal was thinned out and there is now more interior space in a new VW sedan than in a '55 or even a '60. The small-rear-window cars are the ones most popular with those who race sedans off the road for this reason, and also because the initial costs are lower.

Older VW's have some drawbacks. Transmissions are non-synchromesh, electrical systems are six volt, engines are 36 or 40 horsepower and most of the running gear will be in far worse shape on an older car than on one of the newer ones. You have some factors to weigh if you plan to go shopping.

Conditions being equal, a sedan costs less and lasts longer than a glass body on a floor pan car...for a very simple reason. The sedan is a much more rigid structure than the fiberglass counterpart and thus better resists flexing. All-weather protection and "fix it with a big hammer" body panels are also strong selling points for going off-road with a sedan. Keep in mind that a sedan may be prepared for off-roading step-by-step and get you to work every morning during the preparation sequence. On the other

An elastic tie-down strap is recommended instead of the internal latch because lid may get bashed. Large-capacity tank has outside filler available without raising lid.

hand, converting a sedan to a glass-bodied car means that the vehicle is unusable for at least a week or more and it's not unusual for these projects to stretch out over months. When this occurs, the vehicle cannot be used for anything except to occupy garage space. And, you will not be getting off the road on weekends which was probably your reason for beginning the project.

It should be mentioned that the main reason for the removal of the VW body for off-road use is to improve the flotation and the power-to-weight ratio. Sedans weigh 1,800 pounds or more, and a typical buggy with a glass body scales about 1,300 pounds. 500 pounds of ugly weight can be very significant in the sand or mud--yet relatively insignificant over secondary roads or log-

ging trails. It is this lighter weight and better flotation that permits the 2-wheel drive vehicle to compete successfully (under some circumstances) with four-wheel-drive vehicles weighing more than twice as much.

In the sand you will find only one kind of successful vehicle competing. These are bare-bones railers mounting the lightest and fewest components needed to get the job done.

Unnecessary weight is the big enemy in any load-carrying component in any type of vehicle. You want to remove as much weight (without sacrificing strength) as you possibly can and still have the kind of functional vehicle you want to take off the road. Again, depending on how far you want to take the project, the stock seats can be taken out and replaced with fiberglass units which weigh far less (and provide both support and protection against being flung sideways); fenders, deck and hood are available in fiberglass for further weight savings. As shown in some of the accompanying photographs, canvas can also be used as a substitute for metal body panels.

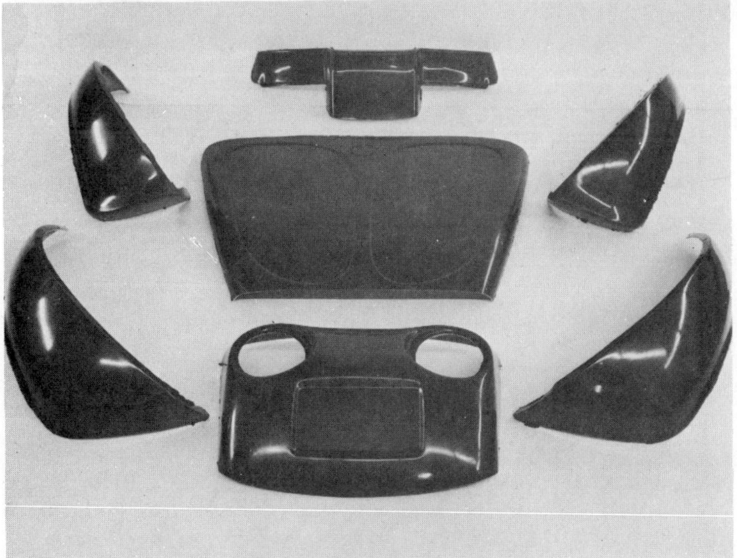

How to lose about 200 pounds of ugly weight: tear off the stock fenders, rear deck and front trunk lid.... then install Miller-Havens "Baja Bug Kit" for about $240. No "glassing" or welding required for installation. Joe Rusz' neat photos of conversion courtesy Dune Buggies and Hot VW's magazine.

Race-ready sedan has canvas hood cover which snaps on, saves considerable weight. Front and rear fenders have been cut back and rolled under for beautifully finished appearance. Removing running boards can save exiting through the window. Tires are Goodyear Suburbanites. Interior is relatively stock except for extinguisher, wide seat belts, shoulder harness and roll bar. Roof-mounted air cleaner is on spacers for air entry through bottom. Car's Porsche engine and skid plate is shown at top left of page 72.

Before forking over hard-earned cash for fiberglass fenders, make sure that your off-road
tires will fit under the fenders. Otherwise, you
may have to trim the glass fenders just as you
would probably have had to do with the metal
ones. This is an area of function and personal
taste. Some guys leave fenders completely off.
Others open them up crudely with a torch and
leave them that way. A few perfectionists take
the time to trim a new radius, roll the lip under
with hammer and dolly and produce a very at-
tractive, finished look.

Most sedans running off the road have the bumpers removed, either before they go out or during
a run. Some sort of curving nerf bar/skid rail
arrangement should go in the front end if the
complete hood is to be retained because it doesn't
take much of a blow to bend it around so that it
won't open or possibly not close.

If the vehicle is to be driven on the street, look
closely at the state laws to which you must con-
form. Fender laws vary and some states require engine covers. Other states have an
"appearance" statute--which is a nice way of
telling you if everything doesn't look nice and
sanitary you can be cited for it.

Further weight savings can be effected by removing door panels, floor mat and back seat. On the
other hand, some enthusiasts build up a dual-
purpose vehicle which leans more toward street
use and outfit the vehicle with nice upholstery and
a sanitary paint job, but still make it off the road
on weekends.

Early in the preparation of the vehicle is the
time to think about removing the running boards.
In rock country these panels quickly get bent upward, thereby preventing the doors from being
opened. This is a bad idea for a hasty exit. If
the vehicle is to be used most all of its remaining life off the road, a supply of eye bolts and
elastic tie-down straps can be put to good use in
the trunk or back seat area to keep miscellaneous
gear from gentle or even violent shifting around.

If you feel the need for more gas capacity, mount
another tank in the trunk or back-seat area--pay-
ing particular attention to include an exterior
vent which gets fumes outside of the carbody.

Jeep or GI cans are not designed for use as auxiliary tanks and are specifically banned from use
in or on a vehicle during a NORRA race. Their
rules say that auxiliary fuel tanks may be added,
provided they are mounted securely and vented
to the outside of the vehicle. The tank must be
out of the passenger compartment unless the tank
has an unvented cap and burst-proof bladder.

Battered and bruised Variant sedan has seen miles of action
in numerous off-road events. Note front skidder braced to original bumper mounts, extra gas filler, guarded lights, full padded
roll cage, steering brakes, padded steering wheel and spotlight
handle. These are marks of a seasoned off-roader. Motto on roll
bar: "you first have to finish."

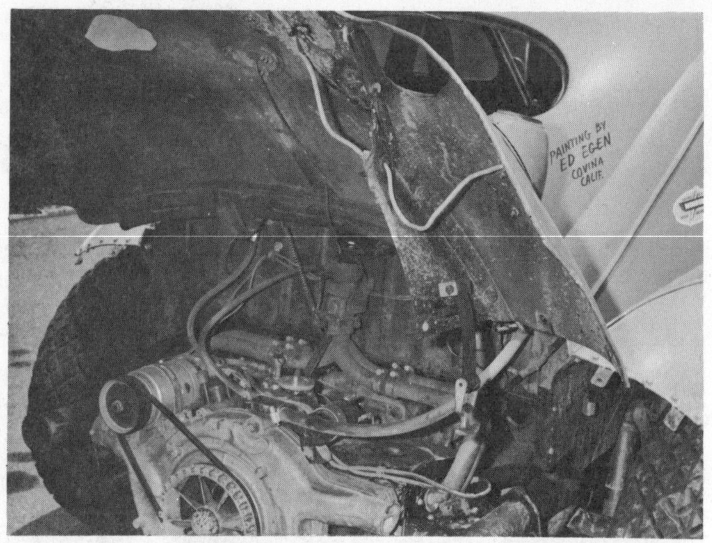

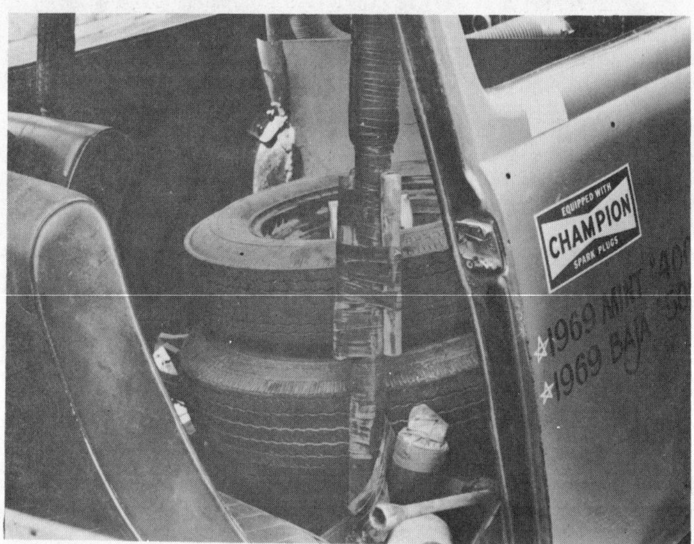

Sedan with flat motor from Variant required engine cover surgery to allow generator-nose clearance. Fenders are cut to hinge with cover for improved engine access. Fuel-injection manifold reworked for single stock VW Solex carb works great. Although you get a large storage area when rear seat is removed, all gear must be securely held down with elastic tie downs or something similar. Roll bars are often used as holders for a variety of small gear that you'll need off-road. Here several flares are taped to the roll bar upright. Note heavy-duty truck latches on front cover.

Body metal can be removed at back to save weight, but if you plan to drive on the street, be sure to check your state's laws first as some require a complete engine cover.

Here's a head turner if there ever was one. Early VW sedan, tastefully trimmed at front and back, with snap-out windows and sun roof. Needs little more than a skid plate to be off-road ready. Car is bright yellow.

Tom Cepek and his father, Dick Cepek, checking out a popular off-road tire combination: Goodyear Terra Tires at rear, Armstrong HiWay Flotations on front. Dune Buggies and Hot VW's magazine photos.

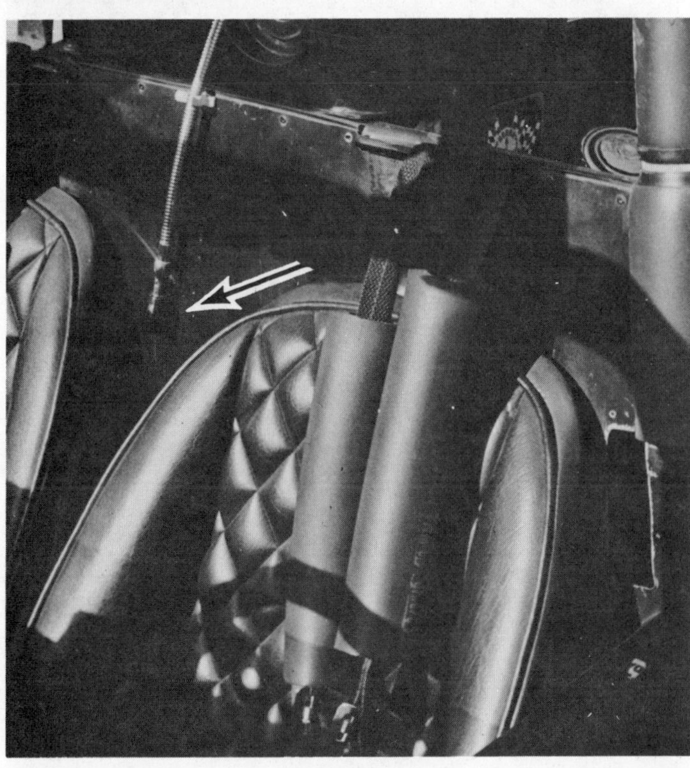

Attention to details can make the difference. Two types of drink containers are secured with plastic tubes for driver and passenger replenishment. Lug-wrench, jack-handle and pry-bar tool holds spare onto buggy front. Shoulder harness with insulation rubber makes the ride more comfortable. Arrow indicates navigator's map light. Poly foam filter-element material covers breather outlet.

Not a welding shop in sight in this landscape. Things had better hold together if you want to get to the end with the top runners. Revmaster Spider single-seater typifies the trend to lightweight single-seater competition for the Baja and other Southwestern runs. Note independent A-arm-type front suspension with large travel. Terry Murray photo shot coming "through the slot" Baja 1000/1969.

Here's that Corvair-powered sedan again — no doubt spoiling for a rat race in the dunes. Fuel tank in the back seat places even more weight on the rear wheels for better traction. Chopping away much of the front end saves some weight and prevents catching the front of the car on steep-rising slopes. Engine close-up photo shows that sand can get into more than your mouth. Detailed attention to closing off or filtering all openings — including throttle shafts and engine breathers — is essential off-road *and* in the dunes.

Southern Californians Dave Larson and Bob Moore took third place with this bus in the '68 Mexican 1000. They drove from Ensenada to La Paz in 31 hours, 49 minutes. Wouldn't this be a nice rig to move the family off the road on the weekend? Plenty of room for kids, dogs, food, fishing poles, sleeping bags and a good time.

Need more information?

Off-road and buggy enthusiasts are often heard to complain about "tight-wad" manufacturers or distributors who won't answer questions for information or literature.

Note the advertisements. Typical ads in the auto magazines indicate that catalogs or instruction sets are sold for 50¢ to $1.00 — or more. But, why should you pay a manufacturer for his catalog so that you can buy something from him? The answer has two parts: (1) you probably won't buy anything, and (2) his out-of-pocket costs are more than what he charges in nearly every case (printing, envelope, addressing and stamps). He really is not in the catalog business — he is trying to use the literature to help sell bodies, tires, parts — or whatever. He merely asks that you help to pay part of the literature costs because he has no way of determining whether you are a literature collector, a discount-house shopper, or a bonafide cash customer.

How about letters with questions? Many questions which are asked indicate that the writer has not done his "homework" by reading workshop manuals, magazine articles which are current, or this book. Do your homework before you write.

Some intelligent questions would probably be answered if there was room for an answer on a neatly typed letter sent together with a dollar for the literature — and a self-addressed, stamped envelope for an answer. Indicate on your letter that a handwritten scribble will be fine — and word one or two questions carefully so that they can be answered with a word or two.

Some enthusiasts letters contain such long and involved questions that $100 in time and research would be required to create an answering letter. Even if the manufacturer or distributor has the answer "in his head" — a typed letter costs $4, whether you buy anything or not.

Small wonder that so many letters are thrown out — or that firms react with undisguised disinterest when called upon for free information. Selling catalogs and literature is an absolute necessity in the automobile accessory business. If you cannot grasp that simple fact of life, then don't be surprised or disgruntled when your requests fail to get answers.

H. P. Books and the publisher do not answer requests for information.